$395   17

Food Production
and Its Consequences

Food Production
and Its Consequences

Philip E. L. Smith
Université de Montréal

Cummings Publishing Company
Menlo Park, California · Reading, Massachusetts
London · Amsterdam · Don Mills, Ontario · Sydney

This book is in the
Cummings Modular Program in Anthropology

Copyright©1976 by Cummings Publishing Company, Inc.
Philippines copyright 1976.

Printed in the United States of America. Published simultaneously
in Canada.
Library of Congress Catalog Card No. 75-28640

ISBN-0-8465-6719-9 Paperbound Edition
ISBN-0-8465-6718-0 Clothbound Edition
ABCDEFGHIJKL–DO–79876

Cummings Publishing Company, Inc.
2727 Sand Hill Road
Menlo Park, California 94025

Contents

To Douglas and Fumiko
who criticized and sympathized

About the Author

Philip E. L. Smith received the B. A. in history and economics from Acadia University (Nova Scotia), and the A. M. and Ph. D. degrees in anthropology from Harvard University. He also did graduate work in prehistoric archaeology at the Université de Bordeaux in France. He has taught at the University of Toronto and, since 1966, at the Université de Montréal, where he is Professor of Anthropology. He has excavated in Mexico, the United States, France, Iraq, Egypt, and Iran. His principal research interests are in the late Paleolithic cultures of the Old World and the initial food-producing cultures of the Near East. Since 1967 he has directed an excavation in an early agricultural village site in western Iran. He is also interested in prehistoric demography and art, and the history of archaeology. His principal publication is *Le Solutréen en France* (Bordeaux, 1966).

Preface

This book is an expanded and partially rewritten version of a paper written about four years ago (Smith, 1972a). In the brief period since its publication, three interrelated crises—excessive population growth, environmental degradation, and the energy shortage—have graduated from the arena of intellectual debate and have become topics of international political concern. It is a truism to state that all these crises are the consequences, however delayed, of the invention of food production. Nonetheless, the statement is accurate. In addition, food production is undergoing a crisis of its own as the three problems mentioned interact with political decisions and short-term climatic factors to produce serious food shortages on a world-wide scale. Some writers maintain that Malthus' predictions are at last coming true and that the battle to produce enough food to feed all mankind has already been lost. Terms like lifeboat economy and triage are becoming familiar.

An archaeologist can offer little in the way of immediately practical suggestions about the emergencies that face us today. It would be eye-catching, though rather fanciful, to argue that mankind had once before, some ten thousand or more years ago, passed through a population explosion and a food crisis, and that we can benefit today by examining the prehistoric parallels. In reality, of course, the modern circumstances are unique and do not have much in common with those of the past. The best the archaeologist can do is to present a view of food production and its effects from the long perspective of prehistory, to try to show how it developed, how it has transformed man and his world, and how certain side-effects associated with it have accumulated. I think this is the most practical and reasonable contribution prehistorians can make to the immediate problems of today; if in addition this book can help dispel some of the archaeological and anthropological misconceptions which often mar the papers and volumes written by specialists in other disciplines far removed from archaeology, so much the better.

While a great deal of interesting research is currently going on around the world to understand better the origins of food production as a process or series of processes, the main significance of the development of food production lies of course in its consequences. I do not mean this as an argument for what historians would call the fallacy of the Whig interpretation of the past. It is simply a way of emphasizing that the emergence of this means of subsistence and a permanent commitment to it by most of the earth's population obviously mark a watershed in the human career. It is almost platitudinous these days to refer to it as a revolution, a giant step for mankind, a great leap forward, and the like. In spite of such hyperbole it remains true to say that it is only with the early food producing societies that we see the familiar topography of our own cultural world appear, and the contour lines on which all later civilizations were built gradually take their forms.

In this book I have tried to paint in very broad, even impressionistic strokes my ideas of the ways in which food production influenced and transformed the more important aspects of man and society, through its effects on such matters as demography, settlements, technology, social

ix

and political organization, the divisions of labor, religion, art, health and biology, race and language, as well as on the physical environment. Archaeologists, being extreme individualists, often disagree strongly with each other on the interpretation of the past. It is not necessary for me to pretend that all the statements and opinions expressed here are universally acceptable to my professional colleagues. In many ways this book is a personal interpretation of one aspect of prehistory, but, having put in a decade of field work and thinking on this particular problem, perhaps no apology is necessary. In addition, because of the restrictions of space, I have not tried to document fully all the statements of fact or opinion made here; this would make a small book meant for quick reading too topheavy. The bibliographical references and the few footnotes I have provided are meant to help those readers who might be interested in digging a little deeper into the topics I have touched upon.

Philip E. L. Smith

Introduction

The idea that a great change came over man and his institutions when he ceased to live in a "state of nature" and became a food producer seems to be an ancient one. Poets, philosophers, and moralists postulated this idea thousands of years before it became a topic of empirical research. There are hints of it in the Book of Genesis, reflecting Hebrew and possibly even earlier speculation on man's loss of innocence as it coincided with the beginning of tilling and herding. Greeks such as Pausanias seem to have had some notion of the importance of the food-producing stage in human development, and early Chinese legends of the first millenium B.C. describe some of the consequences of the invention of agriculture (Chang, 1968, p. 78). Undoubtedly many other peoples in antiquity, nonliterate as well as literate, speculated on the subject. It remained a dormant theme in Western civilization throughout the Middle Ages but emerged again with the Enlightenment of the eighteenth century in Europe. It was a favorite topic of many of the political philosophers and rationalists, and particularly of those in France and Scotland, who used the idea to buttress their arguments for an original social contract in government. They compared the original "state of nature" with that which emerged after food production had created economic surpluses, property, and

larger populations. Buffon, Condorcet, and Turgot
in France and Ferguson, Millar, and Temple in Scotland were among the leaders in this category. However, perhaps the best-known exposition was by
Rousseau, who discussed it at some length in his
*Discours sur l'origine et les fondements de l'iné-
galité parmi les hommes* (1755) as he attempted to
define the transition from "natural" to "social"
man and the disappearance of equality. With the
beginning of food production, Rousseau argued, property was introduced, work became a necessity, forests were transformed into fields which man had to
till with the sweat of his brow, while misery and
slavery grew up with the crops man had now learned
to grow.

In the nineteenth century, the topic became a
preserve of the early evolutionary anthropologists
and of the prehistoric archaeologists as they
searched for documentation of the transformation of
mankind from "savagery" to "barbarism" to "civilization." Via Morgan (1877) and Engels (1884) it
penetrated Marxist political thinking; one of the
basic assumptions of classical Marxist materialist
theory is that adoption of food production had
effected a revolution in the development of society
by changing the means of production, transforming
the sexual and social divisions of labor, laying
the foundation for class definition, and thus setting the stage for the development of the state.

Today, and particularly since the significance
of the early food-producing stage was so successfully described in the writings of Childe (1936;
1942) and a few other prehistorians, the idea has
gained wide acceptance. The development of food
production has even been called "the first great
cultural revolution" by one anthropologist (White,
1959, p. 281). There is general agreement that the
study of the processes which transformed human behavior in both hemispheres when effective food production was adopted is one of the most important
fields through which archaeology can contribute to

an understanding of human society and culture. Probably the only subject of equal significance is the
emergence of tool-making hominids several million
years earlier.

The reasons for this interest lie of course in
the fact that the change bore such important consequences in transforming human cultural and social
institutions and, to some degree, man's biology and
our planet. In recent years, this interest has been
expressed in two forms. First, there has been, particularly in the last few decades, a surge of interest in field investigations by prehistoric archaeologists in many parts of the world. The aim of these
investigations has been to study the conditions
under which man in various places and at different
times adopted food production of several types, as
well as the processes that led to increasingly intensive forms of food production in certain regions.
Second, and in part as a result of the evacuation
results themselves, an awareness of the consequences
of food production has filtered into popular culture.
It is by no means unusual today to find references
to the "Neolithic revolution" in nonarchaeological
and nonanthropological contexts. Not only do scholars from other disciplines frequently refer to this
"revolution;" the idea occurs frequently in jour-
nalistic writings as well. Indeed, futurologists
and others involved in interpreting the present or
predicting the future sometimes suggest that the
changes taking place on a worldwide scale today are
comparable in magnitude and significance only to the
shift to food production in the prehistoric past.
Illustrations of this position can be seen in Thomson (1960, p. 1) and Tofler (1970, pp. 12-13).

The fact that an event in prehistory is taken
as a baseline against which to measure a modern process is clearly an index of how deeply archaeological and anthropological ideas have taken root in
the public consciousness. Although we may feel
flattered at this instance of intellectual feedback,
we should also recognize the hazards. Archaeolog-

ical results are easily corrupted by oversimplification and propaganda. As is true whenever scientific conclusions are popularized, "interpretations"
are not always based on reliable or current information. Even professional archaeologists in other
fields often entertain interpretations that are, to
say the least, of dubious value. In view of the
high turnover rate today in both archaeological discovery and anthropological theory, it periodically
becomes necessary to revise our ideas about the significance of food production in human history and
to reassess its impact on society, culture, the
physical environment, and even on man's physical
form.

Obviously, the cumulative effects of food production have profoundly modified, through a series
of chain reactions, the lives of four hundred or so
generations of people who (at least in some parts of
the world) have been food producers since agriculture "began" about ten thousand years ago. The results of food production have also at times strongly
influenced the remaining non-food producers. To be
wholly logical, a book with the title of this one
should discuss the consequences down to the present
day, for we are obviously still undergoing the after-
effects of the adoption of this method of subsistence. But such treatment is quite impossible in
the space allowed, unless the discussion is to be
unacceptably superficial. Therefore I have limited
myself here to the more general consequences of
food production, and especially to those that
emerged in its earlier phases. Later events have
to a large extent been the culmination of these
initial Stone Age transformations and inventions,
and so they are only lightly touched on here.

First, a word of caution. From the archaeological viewpoint the only areas for which we can
speak with some confidence about the prehistoric
and early historic consequences of food production
are southwestern Asia and Egypt, Europe, Mesoamerica, North America, and the Andean and Pacific

coast regions of South America. In Africa, India
and Pakistan, southeastern Asia, and China, we are
on much less certain ground. It is therefore likely
that many of our archaeological assumptions about
the nature and consequences of food production are
biased, being founded on incomplete or inadequate
sampling on a worldwide basis. Nevertheless, a fair
procedure seems to be to try to define the common
denominators of food production in the regions that
are reasonably well known, and to use these as the
baseline of our discussion. Of course, some of the
generalizations offered here may have to be modified
to accord with new data. The consequences of food
production were undoubtedly not identical in each
region where it was adopted, whether it developed
there independently or was a result of diffusion
from elsewhere. Variability would occur because of
differences in local resources, climate, and topography; because of variations in the kinds and quantities of domesticates available or adopted; because of features in the preceding cultures which,
in association with the local environment, may have
influenced the nature of the food-producing tradition; and probably because of other factors as well.
     The interpretations offered here of the events
resulting from food production are based on three
main lines of reasoning. The most ancient and tra-
ditionally the most popular approach, since it re-
lies on "common sense" rather than on empirical
data, is based on logical reasoning, imagination,
and speculation alone. The dangers of this method
are obvious, although pure speculators of classical
Greece and of the Enlightenment often came surpris-
ingly close to interpretations now widely accepted
by archaeologists and other anthropologists. The
second approach is based on ethnological and historical comparisons and analogies; it can be extremely productive and insightful if used wisely.
Much of our modern archaeological orthodoxy is de-
scended from nineteenth century anthropologists such
as Morgan who used this approach combined with the

logical one. Finally, there is archaeology, which acts to test in the perspective of time the reasoning or interpretations produced by the first two methods, to clarify or in some cases to invalidate them, and to bring to light situations that might not be considered by the other two methods alone. In this paper I have approached the topic from the viewpoint of a prehistoric archaeologist interested in documenting the events and processes of an important change in the human career. I have used ethnographic data generously to supplement the purely archaeological evidence, but at some points I have unashamedly indulged in conjecture based on what I trust is logical reasoning.

This paper, it must be emphasized, is not an attempt to define or describe the "Neolithic" or its equivalent elsewhere as a stage in prehistory. Today there is no real agreement among archaeologists on how to define the Neolithic or just what it represents. For the past forty or so years—especially since Childe resurrected the notion of Morgan and Engels and vigorously sponsored it in his well-read papers and books (Childe, 1936; 1942)—food production has been accepted as the essential criterion of the Neolithic by many, if not most, archaeologists and anthropologists. Other scholars, however, have preferred to base the definition on technological criteria, such as pottery or polished stone tools, rather than on subsistence criteria; in recent years there has been a resurgence of this viewpoint (for example, see Jarman, 1971). The objective of this paper is simply to take what is often, but not always, considered to be the essential attribute of the Neolithic—food production—and attempt to describe the results of its adoption.

Chapter 1

The Elements of Food Production

The essence of the change involved in the shift to
food production is the altered relationship between
man on the one hand and the world of plants and
animals on the other. Thus, as many writers have
insisted, the change can best be understood in ecological terms. Food producers occupy an ecological
niche that differs in many important ways from that
of foragers.

Three factors are involved in any subsistence
or technological innovation by man: the productivity of the new technique, the amount of effort
required in comparison with other methods, and the
degree of risk of failure. Whether or not the innovation will be successfully adopted depends
largely on how well these three factors mesh with
one another. Certainly these factors must have been
intimately involved in the rate of acceptance of
food production in various regions of the world.
It is sometimes assumed that food production provides a more abundant life with less risk and smaller
labor investment than hunting and gathering, but
this generalization is not necessarily true; it may
not be true at all for the majority of food producers. The affluence of preagricultural or nonagricultural societies has undoubtedly been exagger-
ated somewhat in recent years in reaction to the
old stereotype of the hunger-haunted and uncertain
life of the hunter and gatherer, but basically the

7

newer viewpoint is more faithful to reality. The
earliest food-producing groups in the New and Old
Worlds did not always have a more reliable, stable,
or nutritious subsistence base than did their predecessors, and they may often have been worse off
(see also Sahlins, 1972). Food production as a way
of life is not a magnet that automatically attracts
hunters and gatherers, though some of the products
of food-producing societies, such as textiles or
metal goods, may be eagerly sought by the non-food
producers for reasons of prestige or efficiency.
For some, a degree of food production may be adopted
as a means to make feasts more frequent. More typically it is something they are forced into, either
by politically stronger groups or by economic and
demographic pressures.

The old saw that food-gathering man is a para-
site or predator and food-producing man an investor
reveals more about the intellectual climate in which
the idea was coined than about the differences between the two ideal types of subsistence. It is
easy to exaggerate the distinction between the food
producing and the hunting-collecting-fishing (that
is, extracting or foraging) methods of subsistence—
or, in Old World archaeological terminology, the
distinction between the Paleolithic/Mesolithic on
the one hand and the Neolithic and Metal ages on
the other. The dichotomy is not wholly real, for
the gradient between the two is often a gentle one.
The basic food energy resources, of course, remained
exactly the same—plants and animals; the basic
change involved only the techniques of appropriation,
especially through the process familiarly known as
domestication (Sahlins, 1968a, p. 86).

In the loftiest sense, all human energy sources
ultimately derive from solar radiant energy. Until
recent years, all man's techniques for obtaining
this energy have been variably efficient means of
exploiting the energy stored in plant foods, whose
basic constituents are carbohydrates, proteins, and
fats. Man manipulates this low trophic energy store

directly through his own consumption of plants and
indirectly through the higher trophic animal food
chain. In the most efficient cases, man consumes
certain plants that are edible for humans, such as
grasses and legumes, and manipulates the animal
species feeding on those plants that have little
food value for humans, such as most perennials and
those containing much cellulose. Thus man can have
the best of both worlds by intensifying his access
to energy sources through direct consumption and
through the medium of the animal as converter. This
of course was basically what he had been doing since
his origins in pre-Pleistocene times. When man became a food producer, the difference was that he was
drawing plant and animal species further into his
orbit and establishing a closer symbiotic relationship, through the process usually called domestication. A farmer is, to use a trendy term, an ecological engineer.

Domestication is a slippery and ambiguous concept which is difficult to identify in archaeological contexts (Higgs and Jarman, 1969; Higgs, 1972).
It is also hard to establish criteria for judging
whether a society can be considered fully food producing or not. Domestication, if the term is to be
used at all, should be defined in terms of a continuum or spectrum of symbiotic relationships between man, on the one hand, and plants and animals,
on the other. Domestication is often difficult or
impossible to recognize morphologically; its characteristics can even occasionally develop in the
absence of deliberate or planned effort by man to
"domesticate," as with gigantism and accelerated
fruiting in some wild plants, or the emergence from
weeds of such cereals as rye and barley.

A distinction has been made by some botanists
between cultivation and domestication. Cultivated
plants can usually revert to their original wild
state, although by various measures man has influenced the ecology of such plants in order to
further the growth and output of the species.

Domesticated plants, on the other hand (according to this definition), are forever tied to man. Having lost their power of dispersal and reproduction, they cannot revert to the wild state. Maize is a prime example of a plant as an artifact shaped by man and completely dependent on him for reproduction; the banana and breadfruit are others. (Sudden cultural breaks can thus lead to the complete extinction of some cultigens, as occurred in the Caribbean after the European conquest.) Thus, by this criterion, all domesticated plants are cultivated, but not all cultivated plants are necessarily domesticated—indeed, at the beginning of the process they cannot be domesticated (see Helbaek, 1970, pp. 194-195). However, not all botanists accept this particular distinction between cultivation and domestication, and there is growing awareness that it is possible to have cultivation without domestication and vice versa. For some plants at least, the essential factor in producing changes indicating domestication is a shift in adaptation to habitats that have been modified or disturbed by man; that is, the emphasis is placed on ecological rather than on morphological changes. However, this criterion may not be valid for all plants. Again, the criteria may have to be defined in a different way when we attempt to describe domestication in animal species. In any case, there is one obvious difference between animal and plant domestication: although, as mentioned above, some plants may completely lose their power to disperse and reproduce themselves, all of man's animal domesticates have retained their ability to reproduce sexually and hence to revert to feral states provided local environmental circumstances and man permit.

The assignment of agricultural status to a community is also difficult in many cases, even when its subsistence activities are fully known. There are degrees of food production, and the decision must be a rather arbitrary one. One solution is to adopt the criterion of Murdock (1964), who defines a food-producing society as one that derives more than half its total food supply from agriculture and/ or animal husbandry (see also Textor, 1967, p. 73). This is not essentially different from the definition of Braidwood and Reed (1957) of "a reasonably efficient level of food production" as entailing situations in which (a) food acquired through direct production amounts to approximately half of the community's dietary needs for at least part of the year, and (b) both the plant and animal domesticates are no longer strictly bound to their natural wild biome and habitat.

I have suggested earlier that human groups are not inevitably attracted toward food production. Under conditions of adequate wild food resources, less labor is usually required to provide a satisfactory diet. Heizer (1958) plausibly explains in this way the "failure" of the prehistoric acorn-eating California Indians to adopt agriculture even after exposure to it, and White (1971) makes the same argument for prehistoric Australia. The cost-benefit ratios did not provide much incentive for primitive agriculture, which in the initial phases might even have been risky and deleterious to a large population. A good illustration of the reluctance of a basically nomadic foraging group to intensify its minor agricultural activities comes from the Siriono of Bolivia; here hunting, gathering, and fishing are considered pleasant tasks, in contrast to cultivation, and the rewards of foraging are more immediately reinforcing than those of agriculture (Holmberg, 1950, p. 41). Harlan's classic experiment on wild wheat harvesting in Anatolia has shown how easily some wild cereals may be gathered in abundance; a family might gather in a few weeks enough to eat all year (Harlan, 1967). The real economic advantage of food production lies in the fact that progressively greater investments of labor can extract greater quantities of food—both absolutely and per unit of work and of land—than is normally possible by foraging; that is, food production is far more expandable. This is especially true in

regions with good cultivable land, where intensification of agriculture is possible. Among foraging
groups, on the other hand, the point of diminishing
returns is usually reached more quickly. Except in
localized zones with unusually abundant and quickly
renewed resources, including fish or sea mammals in
maritime or riverine areas, greater application of
labor to foraging either does not result in cor-
respondingly higher productivity or does so only on
a short-term basis and at the risk of depleting the
resources.

The most usual, though not the only, form of
food production is agriculture—a broad category which
includes the production of fibers and feed as well as
food. We can ignore here other, less important forms
of food production, such as pisciculture or aquacul-
ture and, in very recent years, the direct synthesis
of food energy. These direct methods use chemical
or other means that bypass the plant and animal converters of solar energy, as for example by growing
single-cell organisms on petroleum for animal and
human food. Agriculture in the broad sense, which
includes horticulture, animal husbandry, and arbori-
culture (tree crops), usually entails the progressive
modification of a "natural" ecosystem by interference in animal and plant reproduction and distribution, reaching its peak in ecologically oversimpli-
fied (and genetically vulnerable) monoculture and
modern agribusiness. Inherent in the practice of
agriculture in temperate regions is the progressive
restriction of the spectrum of utilized plants and
animals in favor of fewer species. The nature of
the agricultural systems favored or possible in each
region depends largely on the range of domesticates
available and on the environmental conditions favor-
ing certain kinds of cultigens and animals over
others. Thus the basic contrast between seed-crop
growing and vegeculture (root, stem, and fruit crops),
being to a great extent based in climatic circumstances, is probably an ancient one, in which the
former tends to encroach on the latter through time.

New World food production was based on combinations of starch and protein cultigens, especially
maize, beans, squash, pumpkin, manioc, white potatoes, sweet potatoes, chili pepper, chocolate, and
tomatoes.   Domesticated animals (the llama, alpaca,
turkey, guinea pig, Muscovy duck, and dog) were relatively unimportant for food or other purposes.   In
the Old World, food production was based on other
combinations of starch and protein cultigens and on
a wide range of domesticated animals, with the proportions varying considerably from one continent to
another.   Cultigens included such cereals as wheat,
barley, rice, millet, and sorghum; root crops such
as yams and taro, vegetables, legumes and many tree
crops of fruits and nuts.   The principal animals were
sheep, goats, pigs, cattle, water buffalo, camels,
yaks, and reindeer.   In the Far East, however, especially in monsoon Asia, domesticated animals were
restricted mainly to pigs, fowl, and draught animals:
fish and plant proteins, especially soya beans,
largely took the place of meat and dairy products.

An obvious consequence of food production has
been a great change and probably a considerable expansion in the range of both animal and plant foods
consumed by man in both hemispheres.   Practically all
the foods on which modern societies are supported,
with the exception of seafoods, are products of the
early farmers of the Old and New Worlds.   The basic
cereal, root and tuber crops, legumes, edible oil
crops, vegetables, tree crops, and fruits go back to
prehistoric times; the same is probably true of many
of the plants providing narcotics, spices, condi-
ments, fibers and beverages.[1]   This applies to animals as well: few species have been domesticated in
historic times.   Indeed, some food animals that were
once partially controlled by man—for example, ante-
lope and gazelle by early Dynastic Egyptians (Zeuner,
1963)—have been "lost" in the sense that they have
been allowed to drop out of the group of encouraged
or protected species.   Some once-important cultigens,
such as einkorn wheat in the Old World and a foxtail

millet in the New World, have also been replaced
by more profitable species. The development of exchanges between different regions and different conti-
nents in the past few millennia has brought about a
great increase in agricultural complexity throughout
the world. New World cultigens such as maize and
potatoes have transformed food production in some Old
World regions, causing great changes in nutrition and
demography. The effect of the potato on western
Europe is well known; the introduction of this plant
and of maize were partially responsible for the rise
in European population that was under way even before
the Industrial Revolution (Langer, 1972). Old World
cereals and animals have had similar effects in the
New World, and the transfer of cultigens from southeast
Asia into Madagascar and tropical Africa early in the
Christian era undoubtedly influenced the local peoples
and cultures. Crops introduced from another region
have served to extend the range of agricultural settlement in marginal or unfavorable zones, as barley and
oats have done in arid or cold regions. New strains
of plants combined with new technology have been means
of expanding prehistoric subsistence and settlement
into regions where food production would otherwise
have been precarious; the extension of cereals and irrigation into areas of low rainfall, such as the lower
Mesopotamian plain, the lower Nile valley, and coastal
Peru illustrates this development. The more recent
opening up of prairie grasslands in North America and
Central Asia to cereal cultivation with plows, trac-
tors, and new strains of wheat is another example.

Determining how food production began in pristine
situations in different parts of the world constitutes
an interesting and ever-popular problem, although it
is easy to exaggerate the importance of origins at the
expense of other issues.[2] There seems to be as much
confusion and controversy about the origins and causes
of the earliest food production as there is about the
sources of the Industrial Revolution of recent centuries. In a sense, the "origins" of food production lie
far back in the Pleistocene and even earlier, rooted
in the nature of hominid and even mammalian subsistence
economics. It is a rash archaeologist who would deny

today that plants or animals were under some kind of
human control or manipulation during Pleistocene times
in some favored regions of the world; conceivably,
even such early types as the Neanderthaloids were ca-
pable of some degree of control. Unfortunately this is
hard to demonstrate, since "proto-Neolithic" activities are notoriously difficult to recognize archaeologically even in post-Pleistocene contexts. Throughout the several million years of the Pleistocene, man's
subsistence activities and associated technology seem
to have been slowly increasing in efficiency of extraction, though not always at a constant rate. By the
close of the Pleistocene around ten thousand years ago,
some hunting and gathering groups were undoubtedly very
well off, perhaps as much so as recent studies have
shown such modern foragers as the !Kung Bushmen to be
(Lee, 1969). It may be that these groups were often
better off and less insecure economically than peasants who live in the same regions today. Some of
these hunters and gatherers were probably familiar
with the principles of plant reproduction and processing and with methods for control of some animal species. It is also worth recalling that cultivation of
plants may initially have begun for purposes other than
food production—for medicines, fibers, utensils, or
stimulants (Sauer, 1969; Harris, 1967). Recent archaeological evidence suggests that among some Paleolithic
groups there were close man-animal relations (with
gazelles in Palestine, deer in Europe, antelopes in
Algeria) that may at times have approached the status
of "domestication."

If we regard the emergence of food production as
an event that may have occurred with considerable frequency in hunting-gathering contexts, perhaps even
during Pleistocene times, then domestication and cultivation can be seen not as evidence of the psychic unity
of mankind, or as results of some unique or miraculous
discovery, but as normal responses to certain ecological and demographic situations. At the beginning,
food production in both hemispheres was very likely
just a regional variant of a whole series of adaptive
changes in subsistence, particularly in the late Upper
Paleolithic and "Mesolithic" phases. From its origin
as an insignificant adaptation it gradually became the

dominant one and has tended to eliminate the other
adaptive forms that preceded it. Not all the early
experiments in food production were necessarily successful in the sense that they persisted; this fact
should not be surprising. In many instances the pressures that brought about rudimentary food production
may have relaxed, allowing the societies to return to
a more generalized or traditional base. The real
watershed in cultural history came not with the beginning of food production, but with its establishment
in an irreversible fashion some millennia later, with
what Braidwood (1975) termed primary village-farming
communities.

Therefore a question as significant as where or
why food production began is: Why did it not remain
on the simple level that prehistorians have called
"proto-Neolithic," that is, on the level of incipient
cultivation and domestication? This is a complicated
problem to which there is no generally accepted answer
as yet, though there have been many attempts. An explanation to which I am partial is that the cumulative
effect of demographic pressures on food resources and
especially on cultivable land was largely responsible
(Smith and Young, 1972).[3] Whatever the final answer,
we can probably expect that there were many more "inventions" of food production in many more parts of
the world than has usually been thought. However, the
number of regions in which both indigenous inventions
and subsequent developments to more complex forms of
food production occurred is far fewer.

A full discussion of the initial processes lead-
ing to the first successful, recognizable efforts at
food production is not necessary in this paper.[4] One
school of thought has argued that food production began in a context of relative prosperity and leisure,
when man had opportunity to experiment and innovate
(see, for example, Sauer, 1969, p. 118). Another
group has contended that food production developed in
situations of stress and scarcity, perhaps during an
interval of abrupt climatic deterioration (Childe,
1936). Surely, this dichotomy is too simple. It is
more likely that food production took place in a
simple fashion on a number of occasions when relatively
prosperous hunting and gathering groups faced an

undramatic, gradual reduction in their productivity in
relation to the traditional work effort needed to maintain the culturally approved standard of living and
the traditional group size and social organization
(Smith, 1972b). Although there is no innate necessity
for food production to advance beyond the so-called
incipient level of cultivation and domestication, various pressures—especially the pressure of population as
already mentioned—tend to encourage it in that direction (Boserup, 1965; Netting, 1969). The process of
agricultural intensification itself tends to be self-
perpetuating, since the gradual modification of the
original biome requires increasing dependency on cultivated and domesticated foods rather than on wild resources. Once a commitment to this way of life is
made, the necessity of maintaining the food-producing
economy transforms the traditional basis for society,
and sometimes alters the physical environment as well.
These successive transformations make a return to the
original state improbable or impossible. Food production thus leads to a situation analogous to that in
modern industrialized societies, where with complex
technology, industrial organization, and an apparently
irreversible dependence on nonhuman energy, "we are
becoming the servants in thought, as in action, of the
machine we have created to serve us" (Galbraith, 1967,
p. 19). Weinberg (1972) has also drawn an apt parallel
between man's social and institutional commitment to
nuclear energy today and his commitment to early agriculture in prehistoric times.
      Certainly the movement throughout the period since
successful food production developed must have been
largely unidirectional. Historical and ethnographic
sources offer relatively few examples of food producers
who reverted to foraging. The Plains Indians of North
America, such as the Crow, provide the classic example;
the introduction of the horse facilitated a nearly
complete reliance on bison hunting. Reversion seems
to occur only in certain situations: when new technological aids to better hunting or gathering (such as
horses or guns) are introduced; when groups of people
are pushed into marginal habitats where population
density is low and abundant wild resources are available; and possibly when, for such natural reasons as a

rapid environmental change, the wild food resources available to some marginal food producers are increased, or (as perhaps in the case of the Norse settlers of medieval Greenland) the food-producing capacity is reduced by more severe climatic conditions.

So much for the general principles and background of food production. In the following chapters I shall discuss the consequences of the new technology in a number of specific domains.

Chapter 2

Demography

The most obvious and perhaps ultimately the most important consequence of the adoption of food production was the considerable increase in numbers and density of the human population. The adoption of plant cultivation increases the carrying capacity of land in terms of production per unit of land utilized; this reduces the space requirements of local food producing groups far below those of non-food producers. Animal raisers require a higher land-to-man ratio, but nevertheless, stock raising is generally more favorable to human concentration than is hunting. On the regional level, local groups now have potentially far higher upper limits of size; on the global level, far more people can be accommodated on the planet than before. Just before food production began about ten thousand years ago, the world may have had a population of less than ten million people; today there are about four billion, and this figure may nearly double by the end of the century, if present trends continue.

We still do not have a very clear idea of the homeostatic mechanisms by which pre- or non-food producing societies maintain an appropriate balance between their size and the carrying capacity of the local environment. Ultimately, the most important factor in controlling the maximum size and density of population is the availability of food of the right kinds, especially proteins, but there are other factors also, including sociocultural and physiological ones. Whether there were any innate (physiological or

behavioral) mechanisms of fertility control operating
in preagricultural times we do not know.

The equilibrium level had been slowly changing
throughout the Pleistocene, particularly in its final
fifty thousand years or so; however, there remained a
limit, albeit a flexible one, on population numbers
and group size. This limit was imposed chiefly by the
quantity and availability of the food supply. At their
most efficient level, foragers can sometimes attain
surprising population densities and levels of cultural
complexity. Among recent examples are the famous
Pacific Northwest Coast fishing communities and certain
Californian groups based on acorn collecting. Archaeologically, there are the prehistoric Alaskan "town" of
Ipiutak with a large summer population based on hunting, fishing and trading, and perhaps, to some degree
at least, the Hopewellian manifestations in the eastern
United States. In addition, there are a number of village sites of the tenth and ninth millennia B.C. in
southwest Asia. Indeed, one can offer cogent arguments that at certain times and places, the pressure
exerted by the size and complexity of population based
on natural resources promoted the first food-producing
efforts (White, 1959, p. 286; Binford, 1968a; Flannery,
1969; Smith and Young, 1972). Like all successful
species, man has an inherent excessive fertility or
margin of unrealized fecundity that, in non-agricultural conditions, must be drastically curbed if the population is not to triple in size in each generation
(Birdsell, 1968). The spacing of children—that is, the
creation of spaces between dependent offspring through
birth prevention and infanticide—is one of the common-
est means of restriction. Among generalized hunters,
where for mothers the difficulties of transporting and
nursing more than one child are considerable, a minimum of three-year spacing seems required; systematic
infanticide, especially of female infants (itself an
added population control measure), may range from fifteen to fifty percent of the total number of births
(Birdsell, 1968). Among more specialized hunters and
less nomadic collectors, this figure would presumably
be lower. Miscarriages account for further reductions.

Food production combined with a greater degree of sedentism reduces the need for spacing of infants— probably in large part because of lessened group mobility, but perhaps also because of dietary changes that may be more favorable to infant survival, such as animal milk and cereal mush. These substitutions for mother's milk might also permit shorter lactation periods and earlier resumption of ovulation and pregnancy. The development of more body fat among the more sedentary women may also serve to hasten ovulation, some nutritionists now believe (Kolata, 1974). Menarche may occur at younger ages among more sedentary groups, thus permitting earlier pregnancies. Less frequent absences of adult males on long-range hunting or other forays might also contribute to higher rates of conception. In addition to these factors promoting fertility, others may have decreased mortality rates, especially of the old: less nomadic conditions, the presence of off-season stores of food, and the availability of porridges and other soft foods for edentulous individuals. Survival of the sick and aged was no longer so dependent on their ability to contribute food. Their survival, in turn, would be a way of "banking" the accumulated knowledge of the group, including medical skills that might extend the lives of the young, productive adults, and mediatory skills that might reduce frictions and prevent fission in the social group. Finally, agriculturalists often regard children as economic assets because there are many tasks, such as herding and weeding, that can be done by children. Certain kinds of food-producing systems may thus select for large families.

Nonetheless, we cannot say that the shift to effective food production brings about any important increase in the average life expectancy of the members of a group. Modern hunters and gatherers seem to live to ages at least comparable to those of subsistence cultivators. There has undoubtedly been a gradual rise in average longevity from the early Pleistocene onward, reaching a level in Upper Pleistocene times that has changed significantly only in recent centuries. Throughout the Pleistocene, as the accumulation of knowledge, combined with the development of speech, gave group-survival value to the oral transmission of

experience by elders to succeeding generations, man
probably increased his postreproductive "elder stage"
of life. This has been estimated by one biologist at
about 25 years (Wynne-Edwards, 1962, p. 601). But
there is no clear evidence that this situation changed
dramatically with the adoption of food production.
One recent calculation suggests "Neolithic" mean life
expectancies as about 31 to 34 years for males and
about 28 to 31 years for females (Brothwell, 1969,
p. 540); these ranges are probably not significantly
different from the expectancies among foragers. Survival into middle and late adult age groups was apparently uncommon in either sex, and the mortality rates
of hunters and gatherers may often have been lower
than among food producers because of the lesser incidence of diseases.

A far more important feature of food production
is that it permits greater concentrations of people to
live in a given area for longer periods. Exact figures are difficult to obtain for preagricultural
periods, although attempts have been made to suggest
density figures ranging from the Lower Paleolithic
to urban times (for example, Braidwood and Reed, 1957;
Clark, 1963). A rough guess is for a world population
of five to ten million at about 10,000 B.C. (Cipolla,
1964, p. 95). Nor is it possible to say with preci-
sion how the density figures were affected by the
introduction of food production, since too many variables are involved. One estimate is that, with the
adoption of primitive plant cultivation, the space
requirements per individual are reduced to between one
and five square kilometers; with the addition of
animal husbandry, the area can be further reduced by
half (Clark and Haswell, 1967, p. 27). The actual rate
of increase in population need not have been extremely
rapid immediately after the adoption of food producing—
one estimate is one-tenth of one percent average increase in rate annually (Carneiro and Hilse, 1966)—
but since such an increase has a cumulative effect, the
results over several millennia would be equivalent to
a population explosion in terms of Paleolithic growth
rates. If we apply the figures quoted in the preceding reference to the Middle East, we obtain an increase
from 100,000 persons to over 5,000,000 between roughly

8000 and 4000 B.C. Although these totals should probably not be taken too literally in the present state of
archaeological knowledge, they are indicative of the
demographic changes that can result in a fairly short
time from the introduction of food producing in a
favorable region.

Chapter 3

Settlements, Sedentism, and Storage

In no aspect of material culture are the changes caused
by food production more obvious than in the buildings
and groups of buildings that now became common. The
impetus toward larger, more permanent settlements is
one of the time-honored hallmarks of agricultural life,
along with a generally decreasing emphasis on season-
ality as a determinant of settlement patterns. Of
course, even in pre-food producing times there are
archaeological indications of structural and occupational clusterings sometimes called villages, including some that go back at least to late Pleistocene
times. This is a reminder that agriculture, sedentary
life, and the formation of true villages are three
variables which are not necessarily interdependent
(Flannery, 1972, p. 24). However, an important distinction should be kept in mind: on the whole, preagricultural "villages" seem to have been rather rare,
whereas following the establishment of food production
in early Holocene times, life in villages tended to
become the rule—after about 8000 B.C. in parts of the
Old World and after 2000 B.C. in the New.[5]

Probably the communities in the earlier stages of
food production, whether they were compounds, villages,
homesteads, or hamlets, were no larger than the larg-
est of those based on hunting, gathering, or fishing.
Indeed, many were probably smaller, and at the beginning food-producing groups were not necessarily more
sedentary than were some foragers. But the essential
point is that, with reasonably efficient food production, the groups—like some of the more favored communities whose subsistence was based on more than

24

normally abundant wild resources—were not obliged
to follow the traditional hunting-gathering pattern of concentration and dispersion, usually on a
seasonal basis. When resources were low, there was
less need to break up into smaller bands. The ceiling on the size of local groups was raised, and life
in the same locality could be more continuous, though
not necessarily more highly sedentary. While fission
because of internal frictions would still occur and
prevent groups from becoming enlarged, the breakup
point would probably be at a larger size than before,
because some of the purely economic pressures against
larger group size were now reduced. The conditions
of effective food production, especially cultivation,
usually call for more clustered and more permanent
patterns of settlement than do the conditions of
hunting and collecting.

Hence, when we discover that sizable, relatively
permanent communities did occur among non-food producers, as in the early Holocene in southwestern Asia
and in coastal Peru, we should not be surprised; we
should instead look in the archaeological material for
circumstances, particularly economic circumstances related to the abundance of food resources, that approach functionally those of food producers. In those
two regions, just as in the Archaic of eastern North
America and in California, the degree of sedentism or
mobility imposed by the available local resources was
more significant than was the exact status of the
foods consumed as "domesticated" or "wild."

Thus the frequent correlation of sedentism with
effective agriculture, though not inevitable, is very
natural. For one thing, sedentism helps ensure that
the sower will also be the reaper. For another, since
food production tends to concentrate plants and animals, through human intervention, into smaller zones
and into niches where the wild species would occur in
lesser abundance, the travel time needed to procure
food can be reduced. More people can be grouped together, and the groups need neither split up nor move
in their entirety from one zone to another as local
resources are temporarily depleted. As already mentioned, this pattern of increased sedentism and increased group size seems to have appeared in some

regions well before formal food production; it was itself probably instrumental in inducing greater reliance on cultivation and domestication. The disadvan-
tages of greater sedentism—the greater prevalence of
parasites, the unsanitary conditions, the attendant
increase in sickness and mortality, and perhaps even
reduced dietary range and increased boredom—were
probably known to most villagers of all kinds. However, the advantages would probably have outweighed
them once they were appreciated—the possibility of
successfully raising more children, the increased security against enemies because of larger group size,
the less frequent need for movement with its stresses
for very young and very old individuals, and perhaps
the opportunities for accumulating more material posses-
sions and the comfort of living in more permanent
houses. Group identification may have developed with
a specific restricted territory—a more localized territory than that used by most hunting-gathering
groups—and integrative social institutions that seem
inherent in larger sedentary groups may have evolved,
such as secret societies and unilinear exogamous kin
groups (the "clans" of some authors — see Goldschmidt,
1959, p. 191). Once these patterns developed, there
may have been a reluctance to abandon them through a
reversion to smaller group size; the system would thus
tend to reinforce and perpetuate itself. The trend
toward larger and more permanent communities probably
did not proceed at similar rates everywhere. In
southwestern Asia, village life seems to have developed
by about 7000 B.C., whereas in Mesoamerica, such communities apparently did not coalesce, if present esti-
mates are correct, until some five thousand years after
initial domestication of plants was accomplished
(MacNeish, 1971; Sanders and Price, 1968). The situation in Africa and east Asia in this respect is still
poorly known. However, long before the end of prehistoric times there appear in both hemispheres urban
centers based on trade, redistribution, religion, ad-
ministration, manufacturing, or various combinations
of these functions.
    Human settlement patterns were soon transformed
in both hemispheres with the appearance of larger,
more sedentary groups based on food production and

dwelling in more elaborate shells of clay, stone, and wood. In the progression from hamlet or village to town to city—the classic trend resulting from food production, although it did not occur everywhere—we confront in tangible form the evolution of far more complex kinds of human relations. In working out various means of using space, the variables involved—natural environment and topography, the critical resources available, social and political organization, the available technology, and the size of the groups—created more complex combinations and networks than had hitherto existed. As in earlier times, the results were usually compromises among a number of needs; but, since the basis of economic life was slowly being transformed, the results in the form of settlement patterns were far different from previous ones. In a sense, the domestication of plants and animals can be seen as a device for artificial creation of strategic sites in places where human settlement would otherwise be absent, temporary, or insignificant, as in the floodplains of major river valleys.

A number of factors strongly affect the settlement patterns of a given region: the individual structures, such as houses and public buildings; the layout of the whole community; and the zonal patterns of communities, in their relations to the environment and to the networks and hierarchies (ranking orders) among the communities themselves. While many of the determinants active earlier, such as drinking water, temperature ranges, availability of wild foods, were still important, others now became of far greater significance in deciding site locations and patterning. The quantity, fertility, and ease of working of soils; precipitation and temperatures in the vital growing seasons; defense against other human groups; and facility of communication and transportation, especially in connection with exchange and trade, were important factors. Later, religious and political considerations also became important in promoting or impeding nucleation of population.

Except under unusual circumstances, when adequate supplies of food are locally available all year-round, the degree of sedentism of a community is related to

the maintenance of food reserves. In some ways, a
more important distinction than that between food
collectors and food producers is that between societies that can preserve and accumulate food and those
that cannot or will not. Probably most hunters and
gatherers do have some knowledge of preserving and
storing food for various lengths of time, both as a
future reserve and in order to obtain a desired fla-
vor; their use of such techniques as parching, smok-
ing, and freezing represent advances over the storage
methods practiced by many animal species. It is
probably valid to generalize that food production can
facilitate the accumulation of larger food resources
to last for longer periods than is possible in most
foraging situations. The carry-over of food from seasons of abundance to seasons of scarcity is one of
the ways by which humans have partially circumvented
Liebig's so-called law of the minimum. This "law"
proposes that population equilibria fluctuate about a
point determined not by the mean conditions but by the
extremes—by those factors, especially food, that are
present in minimal quantity (see Bartholomew and Birdsell, 1953). From this angle, the storage of produced food simply represents a successful way of cir-
cumventing the "law." Grains in particular can be
kept for long periods, especially in temperate climates; domesticated animals, as is often pointed out,
represent stores of meat on the hoof—"living larders
and walking wardrobes," as Childe once put it (1942,
p. 49). Thus, although a good deal of food storage
(which essentially reflects a conscious postponement
of present satisfactions to meet future requirements)
is possible under foraging conditions, it is more
typical of food-producing situations when it is combined with higher degrees of sedentism, of which it
can be considered both a cause and a result. Without
food preservation and storage, no higher civilizations
could have developed.

It is not surprising, then, that containers of
various types are much more frequent in the archaeological record after the development of food production than they were in earlier times. Basketry,
wooden, clay, and stone vessels, plastered bins, and
subfloor silos are typical of many prehistoric

settlements, although they were undoubtedly supplement-
ed by skin, bark, and grass containers that were
probably used long before. Pottery is the device tra-
ditionally associated with food producers, but most
prehistorians now recognize that the correlation is
not a precise one, any more than is sedentism or village life. In southwestern Asia, archaeological data
suggest that there may have been several millennia of
early food production without pottery, just as Morgan
speculated long ago (1877, pp. 12-13); and in the nuclear areas of the New World (Mesoamerica and Peru),
pottery was developed or introduced some thousands of
years after plant cultivation had begun.[6] Perhaps
when only small quantities of pottery are present, the
association is closer with sedentism than with food
production per se, although even here there are exceptions. Nevertheless, it seems accurate to say that
only in agriculture-based societies has pottery developed into a quantitatively important product as
practical containers and, later, as devices for aesthetic expression and ritual symbolism. Even unfired
or lightly fired containers of mud or plaster would
have certain advantages for people wishing to store
food: pottery of such material is impervious to insects and small rodents, it can hold liquids for considerable periods, and it does not disintegrate as
rapidly from dampness as do wood, grass and hide.
Another advantage worth mentioning is that pottery
loosens restrictions on certain types of foods by
enlarging the range of culinary practices possible;
for example, legumes with pods or seeds need to be
boiled to be edible. In this sense, pottery facilitates the expansion of subsistence (see Barrau, 1958,
p. 90). Similarly, such implements for processing
plant foods as mortars, pestles, manos, and metates
are found in greater numbers and exhibit greater
stylistic and functional complexity than those normally used by non-food producers.

But the extensive storage of food reflected in
many archaeological sites following the adoption of
food production should not necessarily be regarded as
indicating a social or economic surplus. Some stu-
dents of the "Neolithic revolution" have written as
if food production automatically involved creation of

an economic surplus that then, through class differentiation and specialization, inevitably led in certain regions to the subsequent "urban revolution" (see Childe, 1950, p. 6). This is an oversimplification of what takes place when food production occurs. The definition of surplus is a thorny problem among social scientists (see Wolf, 1966, pp.110-111), and the concept has sometimes been misinterpreted by archaeologists. Technologically, economic surpluses are often feasible among simple food producers, and even among some hunter-gatherers; but in the absence of external forces or of increasing internal population pressure on resources such as cultivable land, there is no guarantee that this latent surplus will be transformed into an actual surplus. When yields of crops are highly flexible from year to year, as is the case with yams, much more may be produced in a given year than is needed for food; but unless it can be stored for long periods, it is more likely to be used for display or competitive purposes than as a genuine economic surplus. An excess over and above the subsistence needs of the local group usually involves increased application of labor. The evidence from both hunter-gatherers and simple food producers suggests that they usually prefer to maximize their leisure periods, that is, to have a surplus of time rather than of food (Boserup, 1965). Economic incentives and political compulsions are certainly among the mechanisms that finally persuade many food producers first to produce surpluses and then to surrender them to other groups or to classes within the group, but there is no good evidence that this is a necessary or inevitable consequence of all food-producing situations.

Chapter 4
Impact on the Physical Environment

During the several million years of the Pleistocene, the numerous foraging groups around the world probably had very little direct impact on their physical environments. Man's forest and grass fires may have caused limited or temporary changes in the vegetation patterns; he may have aided in the extinction of some of the animals he hunted (although this is still hotly debated by prehistorians and paleontologists, and the human factor may only have reinforced trends instigated by climatic and environmental changes); and the immediate environs of his larger occupation sites may have suffered some degradation such as erosion or deforestation. But with the development of much larger and more numerous communities, and with the geographical expansion of population and subsistence, the human potentiality for environmental modification and resource depletion greatly increased. The first serious deficit spending of the natural environment began. It is probable that some regions were so degraded and their productivity and ecological diversity so reduced that a return to hunting and gathering conditions was blocked even if the occupants had wanted to revert. Southwest Asia may be an example of this. Increasingly, man's perception of the physical environment changed, and increasingly the physical landscape was transformed into a cultural one.

Certainly it is at this point in the human career that man's effects as a polluter and destroyer become evident as he makes a serious impression on the face of the earth (see Heizer, 1955, and various authors in Thomas, 1956). These effects mark the beginning of the first important upsetting of the balance of nature.

31

The clearing of forests for agricultural purposes is one obvious illustration, although that action may not have been very significant in the earlier stages, when populations were small and intermittent or when long-fallow types of cultivation were practiced. Still, such clearing probably altered the vegetation patterns of the regions where it was the rule; at the same time, the increasing need for wood as fuel and as building material for the villages was creating further pressures on the forests. Massive topsoil erosion was sometimes one of the consequences, through wind and water action on slopes or in arid regions. The frayed lands around the Mediterranean and in much of the Middle East today provide classic illustrations of erosion, as do dust bowls elsewhere. Some geographers believe the desertification of the Sahara and of other sensitive drylands in prehistoric times, as well as the recent expansion of desert in the African Sahel and the subsequent famines of the 1970s, were hastened by man's agricultural activities. Overgrazing by domesticated herbivores, especially goats, must have aided the process of tree and plant destruction and soil erosion, even in prehistoric times. The process may have been reinforced as the decrease in plant cover slightly increases the surface albedo (the capacity to reflect solar light). This may have altered local climatic regimes and decreased the local rainfall in some near-desert areas (see Charney, Stone, and Quirk, 1975, for a modern illustration). Other consequences of denudation, erosion, and faster water runoff were increased floodings in river valleys and the silting of estuaries and ports, often with disastrous effects on human settlements. In tropical zones, clearing the natural vegetation sometimes led to irreversible hardening of iron-rich soils (commonly called "laterite"). The use of fire may have created extensive grasslands in other instances, in both temperate and tropical zones.

The channeling and diverting of water sources for irrigation, which represents a modification of the natural hydrological cycle by man, probably began fairly late in the agricultural sequence; it occurred at first on a minor scale, but its ultimate consequences were the immense gashes in the landscape marking the inter-

basin water transfer systems of Mesopotamia, Peru,
and China. In many of these irrigated areas, sali-
nization of the soil through raising of the water table.
sometimes removed large zones of land from effective
cultivation. In some regions, especially in Peru,
hillsides were reworked into stone-faced agricultural terraces, and valley bottoms were cleared and
reclaimed for agricultural purposes. The exploitation of moist soils probably reached its highest point
in the *chinampas* and drained fields of prehistoric
Mesoamerica and South America and, in recent times,
the polders of the Netherlands. As already mentioned,
some of these manmade changes may have altered local
ground-surface climates by influencing heat and mois-
ture exchanges. Thus the increased evaporation following the irrigation of dry lands may have contrib-
uted to the creation of such deserts as the Rajputana
of India; elsewhere, modern irrigation may slightly
increase local rainfall. More ambitious projects such
as the Soviet plan to divert major rivers that now
flow into the Arctic Ocean towards the south for agricultural use in central Asia may, if carried out,
eventually affect the climate on a planetary scale.
Dust particles in the upper atmosphere resulting from
soil erosion may reinforce a worldwide cooling trend,
although this may be offset by higher temperatures
caused by the release of carbon dioxide from fossil
fuels.
     The increased population and greater needs of the
food-producing societies induced a far more intensive
exploitation of natural resources within the earth.
Flint and obsidian were now required in larger quantities for making stone tools; in Europe some Neolithic communities may have specialized in flint
extraction by means of long, deep tunnels and shafts.
Stone was also quarried for building purposes, both
for domestic architecture and for monuments, and clay
was extracted for ceramic and architectural purposes.
Around the Mediterranean in later times, artificial
caves were carved in rock as burial places. That development perhaps culminated in the rock-cut temples
of Malta, which apparently preceded the earliest
Egyptian pyramids. These mining and quarrying activities provided a useful background of experience for

the later exploitation of various minerals and
metals in the earth's crust. Copper and tin were
the first important minerals found in native form
to be exploited. In addition, more exotic items
such as rare stones, pigments, and asphalt were extracted in some regions and transported considerable
distances. Finally, although there is little direct
archaeological evidence, it is likely that exploitation of ground water by well-digging assumed its
first real importance among some of the early food-
producing societies. Like irrigation, well-digging
served as a means of environmental control and extended the human habitat outside the range of natural
or reliable rainfall. This provided greater freedom
for sedentary groups to choose village sites away
from surface water, and also made certain marginal
zones available to pastoral nomads during dry seasons
or years.

Whatever the role of hunters and gatherers in
exterminating animal species in the preagricultural
ages, especially at the close of the Pleistocene, man
the food producer was apparently responsible for the
greatest number of local and universal extinctions.
These included particularly the large herbivores that
competed with man and his domesticated animals. Very
likely this extinction was largely a consequence of
the greater emphasis on plant use; indeed it was only
the acquisition of controlled plants and animals that
allowed man the luxury of exterminating his game. The
mechanisms of extermination varied: the removal of
the local vegetation, swamp draining, stock raising
and fencing, and man's physical presence in greater
numbers (Krantz, 1970). Moas, giant buffalo, and
wild cattle are among the species that have been completely extinguished by food producers. The North
American bison barely escaped in the past century,
and some species of whales and birds may disappear in
the near future. And it is probably only since food
production was adopted that man has seriously threatened the survival of his closest living relations, the
great apes of Africa and the smaller apes of southeastern Asia. Today the surviving gorillas are said
to be in pressing danger because of the encroachment

of African cultivators and herdsmen on their shrunken territories. On the other hand, it is possible that domestication has preserved some species that would otherwise have been hunted to extinction, such as the dromedary whose wild relatives vanished long ago.

Many plant species are also threatened by food producers, more today than ever with the widespread use of pesticides and herbicides in the biosphere. The gradual destruction of the tropical rain forest in recent years by agriculturalists and lumbermen threatens many tree and plant species in that part of the world. Even microfauna such as insects are not immune; it is estimated that of the ten million or so species of organisms in the world, probably more than 80 percent will become extinct eventually as the result of human population growth and industrial pollution (Raven, Berlin, and Breedlove, 1971). It is clear that the activities of man in agriculture itself have increased the numbers, prevalence, and destructiveness of plant diseases, including many manmade pathogens (Yarwood, 1970).

Chapter 5
Technical and Technological Innovations

In prehistoric as in later times, economic growth
spurred technological advances, although the advances
often created new sets of problems or stresses.

It has been argued that the period in the Near
East between the emergence of agriculture and the beginning of the "urban revolution" produced far more
contributions to human progress than did the urban
revolution itself (Childe, 1936). Whether this is
universally true or not, the rate of innovation and
invention certainly increased in an exponential fashion
in many parts of the world after the beginning of established food production. Various factors encouraged
inventiveness, including the greater numbers and density of people and, probably, the more effective communication that exposed groups to outside ideas. But
the needs of the new economic base itself brought forth
technical innovations, especially in the production,
processing, and transportation of goods. Increasing
pressure on resources would tend to encourage the invention of new or improved technology-related artifacts
as more efficient methods of getting jobs done became
necessary and more rewarding.

It has sometimes been suggested that the technological developments that followed food production
occurred because men now had more leisure time in which
to deliberate and invent. Undoubtedly many inventions
were made as devices to reduce work without reducing
productivity, and thus to make available as much leisure time as possible. But it would be as justified
to attribute the "Neolithic" inventions to the existence of leisured individuals as it would be to

attribute the main inventions of the Industrial Revolution of Europe to a leisured class. In both cases the basic innovations were the products of artisans and practical men responding to immediate needs and opportunities, though we shall never know the names of the Neolithic Arkwrights, Watts, and Stevensons. It is with the early food producers that we can see the beginnings of what has been called a proto-scientific approach and the birth of scientific attitudes (see Lévi-Strauss, 1962, pp. 21-25); surely one of the greatest contributions of those early artisans and craftsmen is that, working empirically, they laid the basis for the body of pure and applied knowledge that is science.

Technology, which we may define with Childe (1954) as those activities directed to the satisfaction of human needs that produce alterations in the material world, now took on a different emphasis. Throughout the Paleolithic, humans had some slight influence on the physical environments in which they lived, but in the matter of energy capture and transformation of materials there had been little change throughout several million years. Food production marks the beginning of serious attempts at "mastery" of nature.

Some authors have seen a change, beginning timidly in late Pleistocene times, involving the expansion of *facilities* (defined as things that store up energy or impede its transfer, such as fish nets and weirs, storage pits, pottery, and canals) over *implements* (defined as artifacts that enhance or transmit energy, such as spears, digging sticks, and knives), which were the main technological features during most of the Pleistocene (for example, see Binford, 1968b). What is certain is that shortly after the advent of food production, not only did many new artifacts come into use, but they were often made by processes that were new or had been used only rarely in earlier times.[7] Although chipped and flaked tools in flint, chert, and other fine-grained stones continued to be made and sometimes even improved in quality, there was in some regions a new emphasis on heavy cutting and chopping tools in tougher igneous and metamorphic rocks to produce axes, adzes, hoes, and other implements intended for tree-felling, woodworking, and

soil preparation. Often these tools were intention-
ally ground, polished, or pecked over part or all of
their surfaces. In some cases this was presumably to
increase their efficiency for prolonged, repetitive
tasks; in others, the grinding or pecking substituted
for chipping when the latter method was unsuitable.
Neither the heavy tools, nor the practice of polishing
were unknown in earlier times, especially in heavily
forested regions, but their importance tended to increase sharply with the expansion of food production.

Among hunters and gatherers and simple food producers, the amount of energy controlled is small, being
restricted almost wholly to hand labor. With the development of effective food production, nonhuman sources
of energy are increasingly harnessed. Animals may be
used for traction and transportation, and especially
for plowing fields if more intensive agriculture is
practiced. Sails capture wind energy for water transportation, and the wheel, used for vehicles and in
pottery making, enables man to apply energy more
efficiently. (Sailing boats and wheels were present
by at least 3300 B.C. in Mesopotamia and were widely
known in many parts of the Old World. However, the
wheel, like animal energy, was apparently not important
for work purposes in the New World, although it was
known in Mexico as a toy.) Dugout canoes were known
from at least Mesolithic times in Europe, but boats
assumed far greater importance among food producers,
especially with the development of long-distance trade
and the colonization by farmers of offshore islands.
Although we have little direct information until very
late in prehistory, and this mainly from art motifs on
such things as predynastic Egyptian pottery and rock
drawings, it seems that sizable and seaworthy boats
must have been required to diffuse the descendants of
the earlier food producers, with their livestock,
around the Mediterranean and along the Atlantic coast
of Europe, the Persian Gulf, and the Indian Ocean. At
any rate, it was with food production that man began
seriously to explore and exploit those few regions of
the earth that were hitherto inaccessible, especially
the remote islands of Oceania, the Caribbean, and the
Mediterranean. Indeed, adaptation to small-island

ecosystems, with their small natural biomass, is usually possible only for food producers.

Man-made "shells" for shelter go back far into the Paleolithic in some areas. Durable domestic architecture is not restricted to food producers but, statistically speaking, it is more often associated with agriculturalists. One finds evidence even in Pleistocene times of simple stone walls in some caves or shelters, and rather ambitious huts of wood or animal skeletons occur in some late Paleolithic contexts in Europe, as well as partially subterranean houses in cold regions. But there is no evidence that these structures involved any great investment of time or labor, or that they were expected to last for long. With food production (but not always with it) there appear in the archaeological record the first traces of mud-walled houses and the first use of bricks and carefully fitted stones for structures that apparently were expected to serve for a generation or more. Probably the first mud walls were simply layers of clay placed one on another and allowed to dry in the sun, just as the earliest bricks were probably sunbaked. But later, more elaborate ways of finishing the materials were used, such as *pisé* (packed clay), adobe, and fired brick, with which buildings could be constructed quickly in regions where timber and good stone were scarce, and which would provide excellent insulation in cold or hot climates. The tradition of building in mud and stone is surely one of the most important contributions of the early food producers to later ages, including our own. Large timber buildings were developed in more heavily forested regions such as Europe, and probably in tropical zones as well. Houses of several stories could now be built, especially when they had timber frameworks. Combinations of several techniques could be employed, such as the incorporation of posts in mud-brick walls or the laying of brick walls on stone foundations. The elaborate domestic, royal, ritual, and funerary structures of the later food-producing societies in both hemispheres—the palaces, citadels, temples, plazas, ball courts, pyramids, and

collective tombs—were the ultimate elaborations of the
simple houses and storage places of the early agriculturalists.

Complex engineering techniques also developed among
the early food producers. Although in a few instances
sizable stones were set up in the late Paleolithic and
even in the Mousterian of Europe, it was only after
food producing had begun that activities involving the
shaping, transportation, and erection of extremely
heavy stones became frequent (see Heizer, 1966). The
megaliths of western Europe, including the cairns,
alignments, and circles of Stonehenge, Carnac, and
other sites, and the stone heads of Easter Island are
the best known. The massive stone wall of early Jericho (ca. 7500 B.C.) is an example, if the population
that built it was really dependent on food producing.
The Olmecs of Mesoamerica transported large basalt
blocks, some weighing more than 20 tons, from quarries
50 miles away. The extraction, transportation, and
setting up of these and other megalithic pieces must
have required considerable knowledge of stresses, le-
verage, and perhaps measurements. Recent hypotheses
about the use of standard units of measurement,
Pythagorean triangles, and even the concept of *pi*
in constructing the alleged astronomical megaliths of
western Europe would, if confirmed, oblige us to revise
many of our ideas about the intellectual capacities of
the inhabitants of Europe in the third and second millennia B.C. (Thom, 1967). Similarly, the huge "ceremonial" earth mounds of Mesoamerica and Europe, such
as the La Venta pyramid of the Olmecs and Silbury Hill
in Britain, must have demanded a good knowledge of con-
struction techniques as well as skill in organizing
labor.

Food producers seem also, in a number of regions
of the world, to have developed the first effective
techniques by which the properties of certain natural
substances might be altered or recombined. In preagricultural times, natural materials were for the most
part modified by mechanical means: by cutting, fracturing, and scraping for stone, by abrading and polishing for bone and other organic materials, and sometimes
by charring for wooden implements. The few instances

in which the internal properties of materials were
changed, such as the making of baked clay figurines
of the Upper Paleolithic of Czechoslovakia or the use
of heat treatment to control the fracturing of flint
in both hemispheres, are rare exceptions. But now
clays, earths, and ores were increasingly modified to
produce pottery, paints, glazes, and metals. Pottery
has already been discussed here in regard to its use
as containers for storage and cooking (see also Matson,
1965); but it also played a role in technological and
scientific experimentation. When heated to high temperatures, clay is converted into something physically
quite different, in that it becomes partly crystalline
and changes into a strong substance that will not revert to its original state. This process, involving
a profound, irreversible alteration in the structures
and properties of an ordinary material, may have been
intellectually stimulating to some individuals and
may even have helped promote the belief that much of
the environment could be modified and controlled. The
same may be true of the discovery that copper and
other ores could be roasted, smelted, and made to produce metals. It is possible that man's discovery of
his ability to change the very nature of matter played
a more active role in developing his intellectual
awareness and his confidence in his ability to control
the environment than did his agricultural experiments,
since the latter involved only aiding and directing
normal biological processes, not changing the basic
internal structure of a substance (Smith, 1965, p. 908).
In another direction the malleability of clay—its capacity for being molded easily into many forms and for
being decorated—probably stimulated many minds into
exploring new media for aesthetic expression. Finally,
the invention of pottery kilns for generating high
temperatures may have been basic to the development
of metallurgy beyond its most primitive stage. It now
seems that simple metallurgy may have begun about as
early as food producing in the Near East, in the form
of hammered copper points and beads at several early
sites in Turkey, Iraq, and Iran, while in the New World
hunters and gatherers sometimes made use of copper nug-
gets and meteoric iron. But more advanced metallurgical

techniques seem to be dependent on the technological
and economic mechanisms found among food-producing
societies.

In this category of chemical and physical alterations, perhaps we should include the making of fermented foods and drinks, although some forms of this
processing technology may well have been practiced by
earlier hunters and gatherers. Yogurt and cheese are
familiar and probably ancient examples of fermented
dairy foods important to livestock keepers. The
cultivation of cereals and fruit provided an excellent opportunity to manufacture alcoholic beverages
by converting starch to sugar through enzymatic action.
Certainly this process constitutes one agreeable way
to convert excess cereals from a good harvest into a
palatable and nutritious product, beer; a few writers
have seriously suggested that this was the aim of the
first cereal cultivators (see Braidwood et al., 1953).
Stronger, distilled drinks and perhaps wines seem to
have come considerably later in the Old World. They
do not occur in the New World, where fermented drinks
were common, especially in Mesoamerica and Peru. For
some reason, however, the fermented drinks were practically unknown in North America in pre-European
times (Kroeber, 1948, p. 555). The growing familiarity
of cultivators with plants undoubtedly led to the discovery of many narcotics and drugs for medical and
consciousness-altering purposes, but little concrete
information is available on this subject until historic
times.

Textiles have been one of the classic traits of
the Neolithic since this period was defined in the
nineteenth century. A few instances of twisted cords
are known from Pleistocene sites, and nets were probably in use for fishing and hunting by at least Mesolithic times in Europe. Weaving and spinning should
not be arbitrarily excluded from the repertoire of the
preagricultural hunters and gatherers, particularly
of those in cool climates; the wool of musk oxen, for
example, makes lightweight but very effective cold-
resistant clothing (Wilkinson, 1972). Nevertheless,
textiles seem to be more typical of food-producing

groups. Plants such as flax, cotton, jute, and hemp, animal fibers such as goat hair and, later, wool from sheep and llamas provided materials that opened up a new spectrum of possibilities in clothing, in shelters, and in such arts as rug and carpet making.

Chapter 6
Social and Political Organization;
the Divisions of Labor

Adoption of food production, with its frequent con-
comitant of larger local groupings and more sedentary
living, must have profoundly altered the internal
organization of many of the societies involved. Although such change is less easily recovered or interpreted in the archaeological record than are changes
in subsistence, technology, and settlement, it must
have been no less real. The new social forms were in
fact both cause and effect of many other changes, for
success in exploiting a new type of economy depends
on far more than technology alone. The technological
simplicity of such impressive prehistoric cultures as
the Maya—without metal tools, draught animals, or
wheels, and with a relatively extensive form of agriculture—shows that developments in the field of
sociopolitical organization were more important than
improvements in technology alone. Most of the reconstructions offered in this section are based on what
we know of the contrasts between foraging and food-
producing groups of recent times; they are therefore
generalized. Nevertheless, we can probably assume
with some security that the reconstructions reflect
the principal organizational changes brought about by
the adoption of a new basis of subsistence.

Inherent in the principle of food production is
the potentiality—not always attained, of course—of

44

raising the ceiling on the size of local groups to
far higher levels than under hunting-gathering regimes. Scale effects of the increase in size must be
considered. Just as in zoology or physics, there are
functional consequences of the increase, since the
way any system functions depends to an important degree on its size. In biological organisms it is well
recognized that size and structure are intimately related; the interacting parts vary in accordance with
variations in the size of the system as a whole. In
social systems, "the larger the group of people who
interact, the more ramified their organizational
structure needs to be" (Naroll, 1956, p. 690; see
also Carneiro, 1967). New mechanisms must therefore
evolve or be adopted for performing essential requirements. Among the most important of these are:
the production and sharing of resources; the adjudi-
cation of disputes; the roles of individuals in
directing production as determined by age, sex, and
other criteria; and the manner of recruitment of
members to the group or to sections of it. The last
requirement (recruitment) includes the rules of marriage and the rules governing relationships of offspring to parents and of individuals to family and to
other members of the group.

    In looking for the changes that came about in
the domains of kinship, descent, and political organization with the shifts to food production, we must
take into account the situations that probably existed
in earlier times. Judging from what is known of recent non-food-producing groups, there was undoubtedly
a fair amount of diversity in the social organization
of the hunters and gatherers of Pleistocene and later
times. The distribution of food and other essential
resources probably exerted the greatest influence on
the variability in social organization. Although it
has often been suggested by anthropologists from
Radcliffe-Browne onward that the patrilocal band
occupying a particular territory is the model for
most generalized hunter-gatherers in regions where resources are not concentrated (for example, see

Birdsell, 1968), this is not universally accepted.
The exogamous patrilocal-patrilineal band occurs only
rarely; it is probably not a viable response to conditions of scarcity. Flexible, bilateral, nonterri-
torial organization seems to be more efficient in
facilitating reciprocal access to scarce resources,
especially during periods of seasonal fluctuation,
and in maintaining populations sufficiently numerous
to insure survival of the groups. On the other hand,
it is probable that organization of a different kind
prevailed in situations where more abundant resources
were concentrated either regionally or seasonally.
Here more complex forms than the band could develop,
including tribal forms of society in which some band
consolidation had taken place (see Sahlins, 1968b,
p. 3, and Service, 1971, for discussions of this
reconstruction). Extended families and lineages may
exist among groups with abundant resources who maintain loose contacts in spite of seasonal fragmenta-
tion (Steward, 1968, p. 343). Quite likely some
Upper Paleolithic and Mesolithic groups of the Old
World living in unusually rich environments (for
example, southwestern France during Magdalenian
times) and some Archaic groups of North America had
such complex forms of social organization. The
Natufian of the Near East, at about 9000 B.C., may
have been an example of groups which, with an unusually complex form of social organization, evolved
indigenously into food producers.

Thus foraging and food-producing societies can
have at times similar kinds of social organization;
indeed, some "higher hunters" can have what Naroll
(1956, p. 712) calls a higher social development
index than some groups practicing agriculture. There
is not an absolute contrast between the two kinds of
groups in this respect, but food production did
eventually bring about situations in which tribal and
chiefdom societies became the dominant forms
throughout the world—forms that lasted successfully
into the present century if they were not supplanted
by the state form of organization. These situations

came about because food production made it possible
for more people in more places to form larger and
more complex groupings above the band level. The
consolidation of bands made possible a higher degree
of economic activity and increasingly greater social
stratification by rank as well as more specializations in roles and tasks. Reciprocity, and later
redistribution, tended to replace sharing as the
dominant mode of economic allocation as band society
was replaced by more complex forms of organization.

With the development or perhaps reinvention of
the tribal form of society under food production,
there probably ensued different concepts of corporate identity and territoriality. Although most
mobile hunters and gatherers identify strongly with
a given territory and consider themselves owners,
they do not as a rule forbid others to enter or use
it; the need for reciprocity of access to key resources apparently outweighs the temptation to
monopolize their space. With food production (as
with some well-off foragers) the sense of ownership
may be intensified, particularly under conditions of
sedentism and of growing pressure on land or other
resources. In these conditions, one might expect
growth of a sense of conscious, explicit ownership,
either individual or corporate. Boundaries may be
more clearly defined and rights of access more restricted. Among more intensive cultivators in conditions of land scarcity, work and distribution
along kinship lines would tend to encourage family
holdings of land, with each family possessing a high
degree of self-sufficiency, rather than group control (see Netting, 1971, p. 23). The extended family
household is a very efficient device for coopera-
tively exploiting widely dispersed resources and coordinating their consumption. Village endogamy might
increase in many cases as communities became larger.
Unilineal descent groups might become important as
means both of mobilizing labor and of defending
transmitted rights. What the precise forms of social
organization were in each instance depended on many

factors, including the precise nature of food production and the productive capacity. Sedentary cultivators and nomadic pastoralists might be expected
to vary considerably. It is difficult to make
generalizations which can be projected into the past,
but a cross-cultural survey of some 253 ethnographically known food-producing societies around the
world provides some pointers about the changes in
social organization that probably came about with the
adoption of food production. In most societies which
gave reliable or relevant data, the kin group is
other than exclusively cognatic; the kin group is
patrilineal or double-descent rather than matrilineal; and marital residence is patrilocal rather
than matrilocal (see Textor, 1967). Within the broad
class of food producers there are, of course, significant differences in descent related to the level
of political development achieved, as will be discussed later.

The development of significant institutionalized
leadership and of social stratification may also be
seen in the light of the increasing efficiency of food
production. Indeed, this issue can be examined in
the context of the "surplus" question already mentioned here. Although an economic surplus is not a
necessary part of every food-producing economy, and
although such surpluses may occur at times among non-
food producers (for example, the Kwakiutl), it is
nevertheless with food production that genuine surpluses are widely realized, whether in food or in
other resources. Since unstratified societies are
not usually highly productive, we might regard the
increasing stratification of societies as being, from
the economic viewpoint, a means first of extracting
such a surplus from the environment and then of extracting it from the producers. Ultimately the trend
toward maximally exploiting the new relationships between technology and natural resources might lead to
the societies called chiefdoms, with specialization
in production and redistribution of produce (see
Service, 1971). In some places it might lead to

very complex state systems with stratified occupational roles which, if linked with ritual behavior as in India, produce a hereditary compartmentalization or caste system (Gould, 1971).

Except among relatively affluent and sedentary groups like those of the Northwest Coast of North America, leadership among hunters and gatherers is weakly institutionalized and is usually based on personal qualities and skills. A generally egalitarian system prevails. Order is maintained largely by group consensus. Often, one of the consequences of food production is the development of social stratification and of status positions with stronger forms of leadership, as well as new forms of suprafamilial and supracommunity organization. Thus, Textor (1967) finds some form of class stratification present in the great majority of his ethnographic food-producing societies. Eventually, in the most complex societies, impersonal authority as embodied in codified and formal law comes to replace the earlier form based on consensus.

Settled life makes possible a greater accumulation of material goods than more fluid patterns of settlement, and it enhances the capacity for producing and storing food and other resources. If the population density of the region was increasing, the tendency toward concentration of people in a given locality for longer periods up to complete year-round occupancy of the sites might encourage unequal distribution of goods as fission and budding-off into new territories become more difficult. If the nearby lands or other resources are already being exploited by other groups, communities may not split up so frequently under the stress of population growth, harder work, or social frictions. In conditions of such "social circumscription" (Carneiro, 1970) groups sometimes tend toward specialization of production, with those in more favored locales becoming wealthier and the less fortunately placed groups becoming comparatively poorer in terms of possession of goods.

Some of the disparities in class that arise among
food producers may be rooted in, or enhanced by, this
differential access to resources.

A number of writers, largely following Morgan
(1877), have insisted that with the agricultural
revolution property rights began to take precedence
over human rights and human welfare, which had had
priority in the earlier societies. As a result,
social relationships between persons now became
functions increasingly not of kinship but of property
relationships (for example, White, 1959, pp. 294-296;
see also Childe, 1936; Ribeiro, 1968). In keeping
with this trend, kinship groupings tended to be replaced by territorial groupings, and there was a
change from *societas* to *civitas*—to use the expressions beloved by nineteenth-century anthropologists.
Whether or not one accepts a Marxist class-conflict
interpretation of the food-producing revolution, it
is probably true that a developing sense of property
was involved in the trend to greater sedentism. Some
argue that this, in turn, was partially responsible
for the growing dependency on food production in its
initial phases; and that some individuals and some
families were encouraged by the productivity of the
system to work harder and to plan more shrewdly than
others. Consequently, those families tended to accumulate more resources through preferential access
to the most productive local resource areas (especially land holdings); these could be passed to
future generations of the families and increased by
advantageous marriage ties with other families.
(There may be a modern analogy in the differential
advantages to small and large landholders of "green
revolution" techniques in underdeveloped countries.)
Among many hunting societies, leadership is allotted
to men who demonstrate that they are the best pro-
viders by bringing back more game than their fellows.
Similarly, leadership in small farming communities
probably tends to go to those who have demonstrated
greater skills at production and manipulation by
holding and distributing more property than the

average.[8] The growth of strong leadership might in
turn prevent internal conflicts or at least reduce
community fission, thereby reinforcing the tendency
for communities to increase in size.

The rank type of social organization, in which
positions of valued status are somewhat limited, was
probably rare before food-producing times. As kin
networks became more formalized with increased population size and more concentrated food supplies,
this type became more frequent (Fried, 1967, p. 112),
although the societies may or may not have been
stratified. Wealth often becomes a marker of social
distinction in such cases, and status frequently
becomes hereditary, carrying social and ceremonial
privileges, including some authority. Among nomadic
pastoralists, the accumulation of animals is one way
of obtaining and expressing wealth and prestige.
Among sedentary groups, differential status might be
expressed and validated by conspicuous display and
consumption requiring quantities of labor from lower-
status members, including slaves. In chiefdoms,
where the chief holds authority and status as a re-
distributor rather than as a charismatic individual,
society is profoundly inegalitarian as to social
rank, in contrast to the usual situation among bands
and tribes (Service, 1971). Indeed, Adams (1966, p.
80) sees the emergence of class stratification rather
than simply the development of property as the "main-
spring and foundation of political society." In such
sedentary, highly stratified societies with advanced
political integration, one finds examples of sibling
marriage legitimized as exceptions to the usual in-
cest prohibitions. Practically all the cases known
occur among food-producing societies; the exceptions
are among such groups as the Kwakiutl of the Northwest Coast and the Calusa of Florida, living in
areas of exceptionally rich natural food resources
and with social complexity that approximates that of
many food producers (Murdock, 1957; Goggin and
Sturtevant, 1964). Because of their great capacity
for internal and external expansion, chiefdoms can

in certain instances give rise to the classical
archaic states, whether privatistic or collectivistic
(Ribeiro, 1968), and finally to the early empires.

With food production, too, such voluntary associations as fraternities, secret societies, and
age-grade associations probably became important.
Among hunters and gatherers they seem to be rare,
though it is possible that religious sodalities were
present among some of the more affluent Upper Paleolithic and Mesolithic societies. With agricultural
village life these associations probably grew as a
means of building some degree of pan-tribal solidarity (as against kin-based descent groups whose
demands on loyalties may be divisive to the society
as a whole), as well as for purposes of warfare and
defense. It has been suggested that such associations were in fact the chief devices by which bands
were consolidated into tribes (Anderson, 1971;
Service, 1971).

A very important consequence of the growth of
food production is that it makes possible divisions
of labor (or, more accurately, of tasks) and craft
specializations that are rarely possible in non-food-
producing societies; these finer divisions in turn
accelerate technological advances. Among hunters and
gatherers, tasks are generally allotted by sex and
age. Although there is by no means complete uni-
formity everywhere, there is little specialization
except on the basis of these two criteria. Even within
such societies the duties performed may not be highly
differentiated or sharply defined. The breakdown of
labor according to sex that Holmberg (1950, p. 41)
gives for the Siriono of Bolivia is probably typical.
Among this group, whose economy was based on nomadic
hunting, gathering, and fishing, with a little agriculture, the nonagricultural activities performed by
both men and women were collecting, dressing game,
and burden carrying. The men were the exclusive
hunters, fishermen, makers of tools and weapons, and
house builders; the women cooked, cared for children,
collected firewood and water, and made pottery,

hammocks, mats, baskets, textiles, and ornaments.
But with the increasing importance of food production among larger and more sedentary communities, a
partial division of labor based on factors other than
sex and age could emerge. In the earlier stages the
division would hardly be more apparent than among
well-off hunters and gatherers, but it would tend to
increase as agricultural land became scarcer and as
individuals came to specialize in different crafts
and activities, on a part-time or full-time basis.
Most people would still be directly involved in food
production to some extent until fairly late in the
sequence; family groups and local communities were
the operative units and the foci of group loyalties.
But further increases through time in population and
extractive efficiency per unit of land would enlarge
this tendency and permit the growth of full-time
specialists in activities other than agriculture.
There tends to be an allometric relationship between
population size and the number of craft specialities
(Naroll, 1956). Specialization gives the creative
minority the opportunity to develop their full skills
in a cumulative way rather than dividing their ener-
gies among the part-time tasks of tribesmen or villagers; of course this becomes especially marked when
literacy begins (Kluckhohn, 1960). In tribal societies skilled workers can be only semispecialists at
best, whereas in chiefdoms the specialities, being
subsidized, can be full-time and are often hereditary. A rapid improvement in the quality of the
products of craft specialization occurs at the point
of rise of chiefdoms, according to Service (1971,
p. 138).

   Translating these trends into archaeological
terms is a complicated job. In the earlier phases of
food production, we might expect to see partial divisions of labor crystallizing around such tasks as
flint or obsidian extraction and working, woodworking, pottery making, and a few more. Some entire
villages might become specialists in certain forms of
production—for example, mining or trading—and later,

part-time or full-time individual traders might
emerge as a special class, as larger communities
developed and demand for interregional distribution
of goods increased. There might also be more individual specializations in the conduct of ritual than
in the bands or simple villages, where the shaman was
also basically occupied in subsistence. Similarly,
the production of art forms might become the spe-
cialty of certain individuals, especially as ceramics, whose manufacture probably began as the house-
wife's task, became more important. Metallurgy provided another opportunity for the emergence of specialized craftsmen, particularly when it involved the
combination of different materials that had to be
transported from several regions and when complicated
and arcane techniques had to be learned and sometimes
kept secret. The need for medical specialists must
have become more pressing as communicable and other
diseases (and wounds resulting from organized conflict?) had an increased impact on sedentary food-
producing groups, especially as towns and cities
developed. Probably medical and religious roles were
sometimes combined in the same individual. There is
considerable archaeological evidence for the existence of fairly advanced medical knowledge after food
production began. Such evidence seems to support the
hypothesis that some degree of specialization in
curing know-how was under way. Although one case of
deliberate, successful limb amputation is known from
the Paleolithic—in a Neanderthal individual from
Shanidar Cave (Solecki, 1971)—and there is an
example of a successful skull trepination from the
final Paleolithic Iberomaurusian culture of Algeria,
it is only after food production begins that we have
extensive evidence of bone mending, dental repairs
(as opposed to tooth removal) and the existence of
surgical instruments in both the Old and the New
Worlds. Such medical skills may have developed hand
in hand with proficiencies now required in veterinary
medicine, such as the castration of male animals and
the curing of ill or injured ones. The pharmacopoeia

would probably have been enlarged also to include a
wider range of drugs and medicines, as familiarity
with plants and the specialization of labor pro-
gressed together.

The topics of the relative status of women
(their control over economic and political rights)
and of matriliny in food-producing societies are
rather complex. We can first of all dismiss much of
the exaggeration occasionally written and spoken,
and largely derived from the nineteenth century
ethnologist Bachofen, about an early agricultural
phase of matriarchies, female rule, inheritance
through the female line, and the worship of supreme
fertility goddesses. This idea still persists in the
minds of many laymen and in the reconstructions of
some archaeologists and writers in other disciplines
who are not fully aware of the complexities of social
organization. Although it is sometimes suggested
that the status of women rose after the appearance of
food production, because of women's alleged role in
discovering and promoting plant cultivation, things
were probably not so simple. Conceivably, female
status may have declined in some cases from that of
typical foragers, where women often have considerable
political power and economic independence; among recently settled !Kung Bushmen, for instance, the
women seem to be losing the egalitarian status they
possessed while the !Kung were nomadic hunter-
gatherers (Lee, 1974; Kolata, 1974).

It is also an oversimplification to assume that
the emergence of food production involved a shift
from patriliny to matriliny. As mentioned before, it
is not generally accepted today that low-energy
hunting and gathering societies have a tendency toward patriliny and patrilocality; bilateral descent
is more likely than either matriliny or patriliny
(see also Aberle, 1961, pp. 679-680). It is true
that among food producers of low political development unilinear descent groups are common, and we
might assume that the trend toward unilineality is
one of the consequences of food production. However,

although matriliny is most likely to develop in societies with a horticultural basis (that is, where
the plow is absent and women do most of the agricultural work), bilateral descent systems are also found
in simple horticultural systems (Aberle, 1961). On
a worldwide scale, there seems to be no significant
correlation between matriliny and the economic importance of women. As Douglas (1969) suggests, matriliny has certain advantages for low-yield, egalitarian agricultural economies since it reduces risk
and permits easy transfer of food to the neediest
members. On the other hand, matriliny tends to
disappear and be replaced by patriliny as societies
become more productive economically, particularly at
the state level of political organization (although
there are a few exceptions, such as the Ashanti).
The ecological range of matrilineal systems is relatively narrow as compared with plow agriculture or
pastoralism; with situations involving large-scale
coordination of male labor, increased importance of
divisible and multiplying property (such as domesticated animals) in the hands of males, and male control of the major tools of production; or with the
regulation of economic and political life through
nonkinship devices (Aberle, 1961, p. 670; see also
Morgan, 1877, p. 345 for a somewhat similar position).
In other words, the once presumed correlations between
descent and subsistence are oversimplifications of
what must have been a very complicated process of
subtle change, varying according to local circumstances, following the adoption of food production.
     It is probably safe to assume that with the
adoption of food production the division of tasks on
the basis of sex was not greatly transformed at first.
In most cases, men probably retained the more strenu-
ous or dangerous tasks, such as hunting, fishing, and
house building, and assumed the new ones of forest
clearing, herding, and, later, plowing. Similarly,
we can assume that women, in addition to collecting,
took on the more routine tasks of planting, weeding,
harvesting, and preparing food. These activities

were not particularly hazardous, could be interrupted if necessary, and could usually be carried out close to the community—that is, they were compatible with child care (Brown, 1970), like the traditional Paleolithic pattern of collecting seeds, fruits, roots, and small, slow game. In labor-extensive systems of agriculture, most of the farming work is usually done by women, but increasing population pressure on land may lead to an enlargement in men's agricultural work input, both because the available game is reduced and because the subsequent shorter fallow periods between harvests necessitate more intensive soil cultivation than women alone can provide. Plow agriculture is everywhere nearly exclusively male, and female agriculture tends to disappear when plowing of permanent fields is introduced.

It is also probably true that there is a loose association between women's contribution to agricultural production and their relative status in terms of economic and political rights. Labor alone is not always enough to ensure high status, however; active engagement in producing and controlling valued goods is also essential, and magico-religious powers may strengthen it. The status of women tends to be high when they do most of the agricultural work (as, for example, in aboriginal eastern North America, or in much of sub-Saharan Africa today); they may have considerable freedom of movement and economic independence, with a high incidence of polygyny and of bridewealth payment. The reverse tends to be true when women are less active, as in plow agriculture; here the bride's family usually pays a dowry, female children are less valued, there is much less polygyny, wives are far more dependent on their husbands for economic support, and they are valued primarily as mothers only (see Boserup, 1970, pp. 48-51; Sanday, 1973). Hence, whatever the situation in the early stages of food production, as agriculture developed through time in the direction of greater intensification, there may often have been a tendency toward a lowering of female status as women's direct contribution to food

production lessened. In cases where the contribution
of females to the food supply remained predominant,
male status might be bolstered by rites and beliefs
as well as by hunting and warlike activities, so female status might remain low in spite of women's economic importance. On the other hand, increased warfare and male absences for long periods probably
tended to raise female status, as among the historic
Iriquois.

There may also have been a somewhat greater
tendency toward monogamous marriage as food production took hold, at least if one extrapolates into the
past from recent groups. Not only is there a somewhat greater tendency toward polygyny among food
gatherers than among food producers, according to
Textor's cross-cultural survey, but monogamy is more
closely associated with intensive than with simple
agriculture (Textor, 1967, paragraph 242).

Finally, the possibility is worth considering
that the shift to dependency on food production was,
over a long period of time, correlated with progressively shorter periods of social adolescence.
Among some hunters and gatherers today, at least the
better-off ones, the adolescent period is often long
and leisurely; it is usual for young unmarried people
to be fairly exempt from contributing to the economic
activities of the group. Productivity in food-
getting is high in relation to the work input required to maintain the group in many, though not all,
such cases. Among some present-day Bushmen, for
instance, girls are married between the ages of
fifteen and twenty, and boys about five years later.
Until then, they are expected to contribute little to
the economy (Lee, 1968, p. 36). In agricultural
societies, on the other hand, more work input is
usually required, particularly at peak seasons of
planting and harvesting, and there is often less
leisure time. In these situations, adolescents and
even younger children can make important contributions to the community's efforts by herding animals,
frightening crop marauders, weeding, harvesting,

supplying firewood and water, and performing other
tasks requiring few special skills or maturity and
involving little physical risk. This pattern continued in Western societies, both in rural communities and in some urban ones, until the present century, with sociological adulthood and even marriage
occurring in the midteens. It is mainly—but not
entirely—the increasingly affluent societies of recent times, with their emphasis on education and
training as a prerequisite to successful adulthood,
that have returned to what is, by "Neolithic" standards, an abnormally long period of adolescent dependency. It is tempting, though not entirely accurate, to see the modern trend as the revival of a
more typically "Paleolithic" phenomenon. Indeed, the
return of the autonomous nuclear family to primary
importance as the basic economic, affective, and
residence unit in Western countries since the Industrial Revolution can also be viewed as the renewal
of a status typical of most hunting-gathering societies—including those, one supposes, of the prehistoric past (Dumond, 1975). Being autonomous, the
nuclear family can decide more easily to limit the
number of children, as seems to have happened in the
recent "demographic transition" of many industrialized developed nations.

Chapter 7
Intergroup Interaction:
Conflict and Exchange

Two further consequences of food production are
greatly increased tempos of conflict and of exchange.
These may both be seen as responses to increased population density and more efficient productivity.
One represents an antagonistic expression of intergroup relations, whereas the second, based on economic interdependence, is a friendly or at least a
neutral expression (Watson and Watson, 1969).

Very probably there had been conflicts between
groups (as well as within groups) throughout Paleolithic times, though the thin and dispersed populations during most of that period probably kept the
friction at a level far below anything resembling
organized warfare. The exceptions may have been
among the more affluent and denser groups of foragers already mentioned, where more identification
with a particular territory was accompanied by a
greater willingness to defend it or to attack other
groups in a predatory fashion if the need arose.
The Northwest Coast Kwakiutl illustrate this
ethnographically (Drucker and Heizer, 1967, p. 19).
Raids and small-scale attacks on other communities
for retaliation or for food were probably frequent
in Paleolithic times, and some writers have interpreted the fractures and mutilations on some Pleistocene fossils in this light. Whether the aggression

was due to innate or to external factors constitutes a lively field of debate today, with a wide range of opinions expressed. Zoologically oriented observers such as Lorenz, Ardrey, and Desmond Morris see it in terms of a kind of "killer instinct" inherent in man. Most anthropologists, on the other hand, prefer to see human aggression as rooted in economic and psychological factors, particularly in the competition for such resources as land, food, or women (Childe, 1941; Kluckhohn, 1960; Newcomb, 1960). Whatever was the situation in the Pleistocene, it seems that the advent of food production enlarged man's capacity for coming into conflict with neighbors on a much more ambitious scale. Now there were not only the traditional targets of predation, but also far more loot in the form of domesticated animals, stored foods, exotic imports, and slaves. Eternal conflict between pastoral nomads and sedentary populations, as well as among pastoral nomads themselves, probably goes back to the emergence of the latter form of food production. Raiding is often a necessary supplement for survival.

At any rate, some of the conflict between food producers and their competitors of whatever type may be reflected in the archaeological record. Examples are the stone wall and rock-cut ditch around early Jericho (provided, as earlier noted, that its builders were in fact food producers); the massive fortress wall around Hacilar in Anatolia during the sixth millennium B.C.; the moats and stockades around Neolithic villages in Europe; the stockaded Mississippian villages of eastern North America; and the prehistoric fortifications of New Zealand.

There seems to be a strong association between expanding societies and organized or systematic warfare. In many instances, conflict probably resulted from the need of shifting cultivators to find suitable land, forested or not, in the face of growing shortages and competition (for recent illustrations, see Vayda, 1961; 1971). Warfare itself was

sometimes a means for keeping population pressure
down, as Kroeber has remarked for the eastern United
States, where endemic warfare existed in early historic and probably in late prehistoric times (Kroeber,
1939, pp. 148-149). Warfare might also have served
as a mechanism whereby village mobility was made more
difficult and agriculture and craft specializations
were intensified in the more circumscribed communities,
as is suggested in the conflict between modern Amazo-
nian Village cultivators (Carneiro, 1970). Indeed, conflict between independent towns over land is seen as
one of the principal factors in bringing about the
urban revolution in Mesopotamia (Adams, 1966; Childe,
1942; Young, 1972). The development of valuable
resources, such as irrigated or reclaimed lands,
mines, and other localized property, would have increased the incentives for predatory attacks. Fur-
thermore, as societies became more complex and
specialized in the division of labor, there would
have been a need for additional workers in labor-
intensive occupations; this need would have enhanced
the market for slaves far beyond the level found in
simpler societies, including some foraging societies.
It is probable, too, that the notion of conquest and
permanent subjugation of a whole people by another
and of religious conversions by force are fairly
recent phenomena. They are probably practiced only
by large societies considerably beyond the band or
tribal village level—that is, they are characteristics of certain food producers (Kluckhohn, 1960,
p. 398).
　　The other side of the coin is represented by
more elaborate forms of exchange of commodities.
External economic institutions, including trade
between communities and regions, became more important and did more than merely serve local subsistence goals. Evidence of exchanges of goods,
including some transported for fairly long distances,
is not lacking even in Pleistocene times—seashells
from distant coasts, raw materials such as obsidian
for tool-making, and so on. But it is with the

development of suprafamilial and supracommunity
organization more typical of food producers, especially the development of larger and more sedentary
communities, that these exchanges became institutionalized in the form of trade and markets for both
necessities and luxury goods. Greater community
sedentism meant that the range of direct exploitation for a group was reduced—hence the need for
intermediaries to provide the now less accessible
goods. In some cases pastoral nomads may have
served this function in the Near East by at least
5000 B.C. The well-known long-range "trade" in
obsidian throughout the Near East from centers in
Anatolia during the Neolithic after ca. 7000 B.C.
is one of the earliest examples, although the mechanisms by which the obsidian moved and the nature
of the total exchange pattern are not very clear
(Wright, 1969; 1974; Dixon, Cann, and Renfrew, 1968).
In fact, trade was probably one of the mechanisms
that spread agricultural ideas and techniques so
rapidly. By 6000 B.C., the town of Catal Huyuk in
Anatolia seems to have been an important focus for
manufacture of luxury goods that were traded widely
in Western Asia (Mellaart, 1965). In Europe, certain kinds of flint, such as that from Grand Pres-
signy in central France, were transported long
distances, as were stones suitable for making
querns, mortars, and bowls (Clark, 1952, p. 250).
Obsidian and possibly jade were items traded over
long distances in the Formative phase of Mesoamerica,
and the amber trade between the Baltic and the
Mediterranean during the European Bronze Age is
well documented (Piggott, 1965). It was probably
on this foundation, built up by the earlier food
producers, that the much more intensive trading
systems of later times in both the Old and New
Worlds were based.

Like craft specialization based on division of
labor, the earliest trading was probably on a part-
time basis for purposes of barter of goods scarce
or absent in a given environment. Exchange may

often have been in the context of symbiosis between
sedentary cultivators and mobile herdsmen, where
plant foods were exchanged for meat or skins, and
products from third parties also entered the network at times. On occasion, no doubt, trade also
served as a means of cementing alliances. Complex
inter-regional bartering networks might be set up,
some perhaps resembling the famous Kula ring of
Melanesia, by which such items as salt, copper,
obsidian, and other localized resources were exchanged for natural products, cereals, or such
manufactured goods as pottery. Regional trade networks providing items for local demand and long-
distance bulk commerce involving ports of trade and
specialists might both be tied into the same larger
system. Regional markets may already have been
present in early food-producing times, though there
is little direct archaeological evidence. In somewhat later times, especially in Europe, the roads
and trackways known archaeologically were probably
developed to facilitate the traffic between communities and between regions.

Two of the concomitants of full-time division
of labor and craft specialization, probably at the
chiefdom level of integration, are large-scale production and the development of more efficient
institutions to facilitate and increase exchange.
Chiefdoms typically occur in habitats with several
zones producing different kinds of goods that can
be exchanged; most chiefdoms arise when there are
important regional exchange and increased local
specialization. Among the occupations arising from
the increased exchange are several types of middlemen: the merchants who make the actual exchanges
and the carriers who transport the goods by land
and by water. The specialization weakens social
structure based on kinship and strengthens ties
across kinship lines, while the accumulation of
wealth reinforces the status of the traders as a
class. The Aztec *pochteca*, a recognized class of
warrior-merchants cutting across state boundaries

and acting as middlemen for both exotic goods and
political information, illustrate one of the culminating forms of a specialization that may, in
simpler form, have gone back to far earlier times
in Mesoamerica. An important function of trading
activities everywhere was the diffusion of ideas
and techniques, promoting social, political, and
other changes over increasingly wide areas. Writing—
which in Mesopotamia may have developed in a mixed
religious-commercial context as a way of recording
ownership and transactions and of handling, trans-
mitting, and storing information in relatively permanent forms—is one of the techniques that was spread
more extensively in this way. Bureaucracy was of
course greatly stimulated by this invention.

Chapter 8

Cognitive Systems and Expressions

There has been considerable speculation by anthropologists and others on the changes in world view, in values, and even in personality and psychology that may have resulted from the shifts from foraging to food production. Obviously, data on changes of this kind are not easily recovered by archaeological means, although a few prehistorians have expressed optimism that something of what has been termed the "moral order" of ancient societies may be recovered in this way (for example, Braidwood and Howe, 1960, p. 7). Up to now, however, we have been obliged to resort for the most part to analogies and extrapolations from ethnographic sources. These are often suggestive and can form the basis for hypotheses to be tested in archaeological situations, but all such "reconstructions," including the present one, should be regarded with considerable skepticism until archaeologists have developed better ways of formulating and testing their hypotheses.

Few social scientists doubt that some kind of relationship exists between a society's economy and its ideology, but the nature of that relationship is open to debate. Rather than to assume, as some do, that the economy determines the ideology, it is probably more realistic to accept the contention that the relationship is reciprocal: in the short run a society's ideology can often be inconsistent

with its economic commitment, but in the long run
an ideology can survive only if it facilitates the
smooth and efficient functioning of the economy
(Childe, 1942, p. 18).

In his well-known discussion of the two
"orders" in human society, Redfield has argued
that with the introduction of food production, the
ethical systems of many people who adopted this
economy were bent into the ways of thought and
feeling that are congenial to peasantry, and that
the development of the market and of the city com-
pleted this transformation (Redfield, 1953, pp.
40-41). He proposed two orders that have always co-
existed in all societies but that assumed different
proportions of importance with the food-producing
revolution. The moral order, typical of folk societies, holds people together by moral convictions
on what is right; it stresses morality, conscience,
and sentiments. The technical order includes all
other forms of coordination of activity in human
societies. The bonds are those of mutual usefulness
and deliberate coercion: "men are bound by things,
or are themselves things" (Redfield, 1953, p. 21).
In societies of preagriculturalists and early agriculturalists, the moral order was predominant. It
is only since man became a food producer that any
societies have begun to expand the technical order
to the point where it becomes great—though not, it
must be added, necessarily predominant over the
moral order. Redfield's thesis has some points in
common with that of Lévi-Strauss, who contrasts the
"cold" societies that existed before the Neolithic
revolution with the "hot" ones that followed it.
The former have limited total manpower and a mechanical mode of functioning; inspire in their members
a predominant concern for perseverance; have political lives based on consent and unanimity; maintain
modest standards of living with a careful conserva-
tion of natural resources; and have types of marriage rules that function to set the upper limit of
the fertility rate in relation to available

resources. In "hot" societies, on the other hand, the unceasingly greater demands for energy extraction lead to differentiation and opposition between classes and between castes, culminating in the city-states of many parts of the world based on unequal statuses between dominant and dominated groups (Lévi-Strauss, 1966).

Such interpretations by social anthropologists, like many of those by earlier political philosophers, are based on analogies from recent peoples and are artifacts of the theoretical models favored by the interpreters. Archaeologists often feel uncomfortable when offered such views; some may see such offerings as attempts at practicing paleo-psychology without a license. Nevertheless, the dominant attitudes and values of foragers can often differ considerably from those of food producers, and it is legitimate to postulate that the attitudes of the latter are largely products of the adoption of effective food production since the end of Pleistocene times. Redfield saw the moral order of peasants as characterized by a pattern of dominant attitudes emphasizing a practical, utilitarian view toward nature, yet with work seen not only as materially productive but also as a fulfillment of divine command. There is a de-emphasis of emotion, a concern with security rather than with adventure, a high valuation of procreation and of children, a desire for wealth, and the joining of social justice with work as basic ethical notions (Redfield, 1953, pp. 38-39). Kluckhohn, who was in basic agreement with Redfield, has discussed this subject in the context of the relationship between the size of social groups and the characteristics of their value systems since food production began. He argues that in situations where fundamental interpersonal relations are no longer on a face-to-face basis or predominantly those of kin groups, the moral order as described by Redfield is more inclusive. In addition, there is a sharpening of the demarcation between self and non-self; ideas take their place as forces in history as

contact increases with groups having contrasting
moral orders (and hence the need to justify and even
codify the existing moral order); and systematic
armed warfare leads ultimately not only to conquest
and permanent subjugation of other peoples, but also,
perhaps, to doctrines of the brotherhood of all mankind (Kluckhohn, 1960).

Even more explicit attempts have been made to
distinguish the different modal personality types of
foragers and food producers, based on the assumption
that the demands of existence and survival will
create such different types. Lewis Mumford has
speculated on this distinction as reflected in the
tools of prehistoric man. He suggests that the
"dynamic, imaginative, audacious, violent, custom-
breaking" psychology of hunters and gatherers is
reflected in the swift snapping of Paleolithic tools.
This is in contrast to the "good, sober, industrious,
utilitarian, life-oriented neolithic villagers [who]
were probably a little deficient in imagination"
and who had a greater tolerance for grinding (Mumford, 1960, pp. 227-228, 232). This is an exagger-
ated dichotomy, of course, because food producers
often make excellent chipped and snapped stone tools,
and hunters and gatherers have been known to manufacture some very pedestrian stone implements—
including, at times, ground and polished stone ones.
Nevertheless, the general contrasts between the
material products of the two ideal economic forms
may be more than simple coincidence. Food production does involve long-range planning for future
needs and perhaps more experimentation on a trial-
and-error basis; hunting is often based on tactics
(that is, short-range decisions) rather than on
strategy. Over a long period of time, this difference may have given a selective advantage to a
different range of temperaments, where indirection,
patience, and even stolidity were more adaptive than
such qualities as rapid decision making or a liking
for novelty. As Netting recently expressed it,
"there is probably something to the notion that

there is a peasant personality, but we are still a
long way from being able to demonstrate it" (1974,
p. 36).

One might also argue that the time perspective
of established food producers is different from
that of most hunters and gatherers. Stock breeding
and plant selection involve long-term processes that
postpone immediate satisfactions; their success may
involve years or even lifetimes of work. The gradual elaboration of architectural forms that were
meant to last for more than one or a few seasons is
an illustration of this enlarged time perspective.
Another prehistorian has suggested that food production, especially stock breeding, encourages an
emphasis on lineality of descent and thus on the
maintenance of long human genealogies. This in
turn promotes a sense of the lineality of the past
and future in the conceptual horizons of the group
(Clark, 1966). A practical consequence of this
attitude, if it required forecasting in the economic
and religious spheres and synchronization of efforts,
might be the elaboration of directional or quantitative measures for time, such as calendars.[9] In this
respect one thinks of the "observatories" and even
megalithic "computers" for marking the summer and
winter solstices or the equinoxes that some astron-
omers have suggested as the functions of such
European monuments as Stonehenge and Carnac
(Hawkins, 1965). Up to now, these interpretations
have not been generally accepted by prehistoric
archaeologists. However, even though some monuments
have doubtlessly been misunderstood by the astron-
omers, there is no reason to discard completely the
idea of fairly advanced calculations by food-
producing tribal or chiefdom societies (see also
Thom, 1967). The Maya calendar probably had its
origin in some such context—perhaps from an earlier
Olmec source to provide calendrical computations
for agricultural purposes (Hatch, 1971). Eventually,
in a few societies, writing developed as a means of
recording present needs, especially commercial ones,

and of recording the events of the past. A marginal
offshoot of astronomical—or rather, astrological—
activities was the invention of the zodiac, whose
signs acquired prophetic significance. Its modern
popularity attests to its enduring attraction through
many thousands of years.

Speculations such as these on the attitudes that
may have emerged or became more significant with the
advent of food production are strengthened by ethnographic studies of the differences in emphasis in
child-rearing practices among a sample of hunting-
gathering and food-producing groups around the world
(Barry, Child, and Bacon, 1959). The investigations
were concerned with the degree to which parents put
pressure on their offspring in such matters as compliance, achievement, self-reliance, and independence.
Of the hunting-gathering sample, the overwhelming
majority (80 percent) stressed assertiveness more
than compliance, whereas about the same proportion
of food producers stressed compliance over assertiveness. An explanation is that since foragers have no
"investment" to protect, independence and assertiveness are valued from childhood; but food producers
have domesticated animals and fields, which even
young children can guard under threat of punishment;
therefore responsibility and obedience are stressed
as values. A contributing factor may be the types
of play groups, judging from recent studies of !Kung
Bushmen, both hunting-gathering nomads and sedentar-
ized food producers. In the small nomadic groups,
children of all ages and both sexes play together,
so real competition is made difficult. Among the
larger, settled groups, there is stricter segrega-
tion of play groups by age and by sex, and aggres-
siveness in play is more frequent and more tolerated
by elders (Kolata, 1974). Holmberg's ethnographic
description of Siriono personality (1950, p. 98) and
his explanation for it certainly agree well with
this generalization as applied to a basically hunting-
gathering group in another part of the world.
Although archaeologists find it virtually impossible

to document or demonstrate such subtle shifts as
these in the pots, flints, and bricks they study,
the changes were undoubtedly taking place all the
same in many early food-producing societies.

There have also been a few attempts to explain
the total philosophical orientation of a society or
group of societies, not simply in terms of food production as compared with foraging, but in terms of
the kinds of domesticated foods present and man's
attitudes toward them. Thus it has been suggested
that economies derived from the Near East, based on
hard grains and herd animals that require direct,
selective, and positive action by man, result in an
"interventionist" mentality. This is associated
with an emphasis on the shepherd-flock or God-man
attitude in religion and society and a bias toward
slave-based and later capitalistic modes of production. In the Far East and Oceania, on the other
hand, domesticated herd animals are of little importance; agriculture is based largely on cultivated
root and rhizome crops that are propagated by trans-
planted cuttings, requiring a different, more
intimate relationship to the plant. The result in
terms of human attitudes is seen as nonintervention-
ist and indirect, with a tendency to see the relations between men in terms of plant symbols (Haudricourt, 1970). Although this kind of correlation can
easily be criticized for gross oversimplification,
it nevertheless points to an area of causality that
has not so far received much attention from anthropologists.

But perhaps on a more concrete level the
presence or absence of certain species is influential
in molding not only the subsistence and settlement
style, but even the cultural history of a region or
continent. Well known are the effects of the predatory nomadic pastoral chiefdoms in the Old World—
Hyksos, Huns, Mongols, and Arabs—as they came into
conflict with more sedentary groups and played a
dynamic role in the evolutionary process; there
must have been many analogous cases in prehistoric

times. Probably where pastoral peoples were absent
because there were no animals suitable for riding
or traction, as was true in most of the Americas,
cultural and social evolution took a slower and
perhaps less tumultuous form (Ribeiro, 1968, pp.
143-144). Similarly, where domesticated animals
are present, they are used not only for food and
traction, but also as symbols of wealth, prestige,
and religious belief, for aesthetic pleasure, and
for verbal symbolism in the myths, songs, and
vocabulary of the societies possessing them. One
has only to think of cattle in India and Africa,
sheep in Middle Eastern tradition and mythology,
the lamb, dove, and pigeon in Christian iconography
and symbolism, and of the role of animals in the
religious pantheon of ancient Egypt to appreciate
this point. Of course, some plants and animals
may originally have been brought under control for
ceremonial, religious, or aesthetic reasons rather
than for purely economic ones, as many writers have
argued since at least the nineteenth century (Sauer,
1969; Isaac, 1970).

Probably very closely linked to changes in
moral order and world view are changes in the
religious views and expressions of those groups
adopting food production. Here again we are on
very precarious ground, for the archaeological
materials are usually ambiguous. The classical
viewpoint, still expressed in popular and even in
some professional writings, is that whereas hunters
are interested primarily in the fertility of their
game, food producers are mainly interested in their
own fertility and in that of their domesticated food
sources. Hence, with food production there is more
emphasis on rain and wind spirits, sun and moon
deities, and particularly "Earth Mother Goddesses."
Since we know little with certainty about the forms
or content of religion among the preagriculturalists,
such statements are hard to evaluate. The agricultural cycle of food producers, involving annual
renewals of plants and herds, probably did provide

a stronger focus of group beliefs, as expressed in agricultural cults hallowing aspects of sunlight, wind, rain, and water. There has been little archaeological success in demonstrating the reality of the supposed development of religious belief and attitudes through time—for example, the old Frazerian hypothesis that magical and fertility rituals among early food producers involved actors who became "corn kings" and later secular kings (see Childe, 1942, p. 65). The items encountered by archaeologists in early food-producing sites, such as clay animals and human figurines, or "shrines" containing animal or human skulls, may be interpreted as reflections of belief in the efficacy of fertility rites. But, of course, they may have other meanings entirely.

Some historians of religion have argued that with the invention of agriculture the old ideas linking the fecundity of the earth with female mystery and sexuality, blood sacrifice, and rituals of death and resurrection were now charged with new values and articulated in new patterns—a "religious revolution" for one writer (Isaac, 1970). According to some writers, a mystical solidarity developed between man and plant life, and to ensure the life of the nutritive plants, human and animal sacrifice was instituted and ritualized around the idea of periodic renewal of cosmic sacrality. There was increased antagonism between the sexes; the cult of the dead became more important; there was a greater interest in supreme gods and creators, in sovereign or warrior gods, and, among many pastoral peoples, in celestial deities (for example, see Campbell, 1959; Eliade, 1960). These interpretations are probably too specific to find favor with most anthropologists, who nevertheless would agree that, as the technological and economic bases for societies change, the philosophical and religious expressions of experience will also change. But the problem of distinguishing cause from effect is a difficult one. The more modest extrapolations of writers such as Kluckhohn

(1960) are probably more willingly accepted: that with the expanding society following the establishment of food production, the moral order is more internalized and projected into the life after death; nature and the cosmos are somewhat less personalized or humanized; and a full-time priesthood may develop as external enforcement of the moral order becomes more impersonal and bureaucratic. It has also been argued that as one moves toward societies with greater economic surplus, social complexity, and status inequality, there is a decrease in the relative importance of private or individualistically defined religious experiences (Albers and Parker, 1971). Here again, it is necessary to distinguish among food producers between cultivators and nomads; the latter, at least today, tend to favor stoical and unritualized relationships between man and an omnipotent environment rather than institutionalized religion linked to an anthropomorphic cosmos (Spooner, 1973, p. 41).

Whatever the precise orientation of the cosmology and belief, the possibilities inherent in food production for the accumulation of large quantities of goods, for specialization of vocations, and for community growth were in themselves sufficient to ensure the later emergence in both hemispheres of highly formalized religious structures and temple hierarchies. Such structures, if not themselves theocratic in nature, often provided support for a ruling class that controlled a large subordinate majority. "Living gods" could hardly be possible in hunting-gathering or even simple food-producing societies. The development of ceremonial-religious complexes would in turn reinforce the social system and to some degree the economic system and its related technology; the temple organization served in some cases (for example, in Mesopotamia) as centers of redistribution of local goods and as agents of communication and trade with external groups. Some authors refer to such an organization as the state-church and attribute to it a powerful function in coordinating and integrating the various occupational groups that had now arisen (see White, 1959, p. 301). Long before this, however, ideologies of descent may have developed, paired with religious belief, to validate family or group ownership of resources, especially of land. The ancestors were considered as continuing participants in the affairs of the descent group, and the dead were buried, sometimes collectively, under the residences or in the owned land. The beginnings of this trend can perhaps be seen in the appearance of the first true cemeteries even before food production began, in the late Paleolithic-Mesolithic of the Old World and the Archaic of the New World. With food production such an ideology could become magnified and elaborated.

It is also worth considering that if, as already suggested, the beginning of a scientific mental attitude goes back to the early food-producing stage, then with the increasingly evident profitability of this approach, the parallel expression known as magic lessened in importance. Science and magic are both articulated systems; they are two parallel modes of knowledge. However, as Lévi-Strauss has emphasized (1962, pp. 21-23), the former has a greater capacity for profitable and practical results that might in the long run have favored in some societies a greater reliance on observation and on bold, controlled hypotheses, without completely eliminating the latter mode. In the long run, science has tended to replace magic as a way of controlling or exploiting nature; magic of one kind or another still, however, retains its function as a means of manipulating people.

Does food production result in new and different expressions and meaning in art? Some authors have believed that it does, and the viewpoint is completely defensible. Childe suggested that, unlike Paleolithic artists, the Neolithic peasants never tried to depict animals, humans, and other natural objects (Childe, 1950, 1953). But the contention that art showed a shift from naturalism

to abstraction (an idea that basically goes back
to nineteenth-century evolutionist anthropology)
is true only if we take European events as the measure. Even then there are many exceptions: the
Upper Paleolithic art of eastern Europe and the
Ukraine is largely unnaturalistic, as is much of
both Mesolithic art and aboriginal Australian art,
whereas the art of such Neolithic sites as Chatal
Huyuk in Anatolia and the paintings and engravings
of the early pastoralists of the Sahara are very
naturalistic at times.

In actual fact, it is difficult to say just
what changes in style or meaning we can attribute to
the introduction of food production. It is particularly so in regions such as southwestern Asia where,
although there seems to have been cultural contin-
uity from foragers to food producers, we have little
knowledge of what kinds of art were practiced before
food production began. Obviously, some new techniques were now available. Murals could be painted
on the plastered walls of buildings, pottery provided another working surface, and the plastic
qualities of clay opened up far more opportunities
than had been known in earlier times. The development of textiles, particularly for personal wear,
and of rugs, hangings, and carpets provided an
aesthetic outlet for many sedentary peoples, but
especially for nomadic herdsmen, for whom lightness,
portability, and flexibility in material culture is
important. This pattern has continued in western
and central Asia to the present day. Metallurgy
offered still further opportunities, as the famous
bronzes and other metalwork of Africa, western Asia,
China, and South America attest. Monumental stone
sculptures of humans develop, perhaps sometimes as
portraits, and stone stelae appear in some regions.
The domestic and public architecture which tended
to proliferate along with the development of food
production must be seen not only as functional
objects and as codifications of social and religious

patterns, but also as expressions of aesthetic canons.

On a less tangible level we might even entertain the idea—without holding out much hope of archaeological proof— that there were some changes in the nature and content of songs and dances as food production evolved. At least one pair of writers sees increases in the explicitness or information load of songs as economic productivity and political centralization increase. These latter aspects are in turn linked to other changes in division of labor, group organization, and group cohesiveness (Lomax and Berkowitz, 1972). Finally, we can even speculate that—since food itself is an art form with very clear aesthetic functions in addition to its nutritional one, and governed by rigorously formalized sets of rules which can even be seen as summations of the symbolic systems of the societies involved (Douglas, 1974)—then this realm of art may also have expanded and intensified as food production and food-producing societies developed.

Like religion, art was undoubtedly closely tied in with the general and specific changes in ideology and attitudes that accompanied the advent of food production. Nonetheless, it remains difficult to state any valid generalization or regularity. The relationship between the art and the economy of a given group is not necessarily direct, for between the economic relationship and the styles of art there intervene ideologies and social values that affect the chief themes of art as they do religion and mythology. This is another field in which prehistoric archaeology can hope eventually to make a considerable contribution to the solution of an important problem that ethnographers, historians of art, and others have tackled in their own ways.

Chapter 9
Human Health and Biology

The main emphasis in this paper has been on the social and cultural consequences of food production, but we must keep in mind that there were also implications for man as a physical organism. And since subtle interrelationships probably existed between biological, social, and cultural variables, a brief discussion of human health and biology is worthwhile here.

We have a considerable literature dealing with the effects and possible effects of food production on man's health and physique. There is especially a great deal written on the subject of the greater prevalence of some diseases (see Brothwell, 1969; Cockburn, 1971; Dunn, 1968; Polgar, 1964). Some of the conclusions reached are based on studies of human skeletal or tissue materials, but much else is deduced by contrasting life in recent foraging and food-producing groups.

Preagricultural hunters, gatherers, and fishermen undoubtedly had their share of diseases and infections caused by parasites and other factors, but it is doubtful that contagious diseases or epidemics were very important where the population was small, dispersed, and mobile. Diseases during the Pleistocene, except among the relatively sedentary groups that may have existed here and there, were probably caused chiefly by pathogens whose life

histories insured maintenance and dispersal, such as
malaria and yellow fever. There seems to be general
agreement that the development of new living conditions that often accompanied food production, especially greater regional and local population density
and closer man-to-man contacts, was instrumental in
increasing the number of infections—though infections
do not always lead to disease, nor disease to death.
Infectious diseases requiring minimum host populations could now thrive, especially the "acute community infections" such as cholera, smallpox, mumps,
measles, chicken pox, rubella, influenza, and polio-
myelitis (Cockburn, 1971; Black, 1975). Man's
activities in changing the natural environment and
in creating new, larger, and more sedentary communities while adopting new subsistence bases were
largely instrumental in bringing about this state
of affairs. Forest clearing, utilization of wet
soils, and creation of large surfaces of stagnant
water encouraged mosquitoes and other insects and
consequently such diseases as malaria, yellow fever,
dengue, scrub typhus, and sleeping sickness. Thus,
early Neolithic skeletons at sites in Anatolia,
Cyprus, and Greece already show considerable evidence
of sicklemia or thalassemia related to increased
exposure to malaria (Angel, 1966). Even in prehistoric times, the development of irrigation probably
increased the incidence of schistosomiasis (bilhar-
ziasis), a debilitating intestinal and urinary disease
communicated by an aquatic snail that proliferates
in canals.
     Sedentary communities undoubtedly created more
unsanitary conditions than were the rule in Paleolithic times and encouraged parasites, bacilli and
streptococci; it is usually less easy to abandon a
village with more permanent houses than a campsite
when disease strikes. Some of the resulting diseases were bubonic plague, leprosy, hookworm, and
bacillary dysentery, which might be caused by gar-
bage and human excreta, by close contact with animal
carriers, and by rodents, cockroaches, and other

parasitical vermin infesting houses and storage
places. Domesticated animals, through their milk,
hair, skin, and tissues, are also vehicles for passing various diseases on to man, such as anthrax,
bovine turberculosis, and trypanosomiasis. Probably,
over many generations, a form of immunity to many of
the communicable diseases such as measles developed
in some populations, just as sicklemia evolved by
selective pressure through increased frequency of
an adaptive gene among populations exposed to malaria
in Africa.

        Studies of some existing hunter-gatherers suggest
that, far from being ill-nourished, they may enjoy
well-balanced diets with fewer deficiencies than their
food-producing contemporaries in certain vitamins and
in such minerals as iron. There may also be fewer
degenerative diseases of old age, such as high blood
pressure; many !Kung Bushmen live to sixty, and some
even to eighty years (Kolata, 1974). Thus a shift
to food production may not automatically bring about
better nutrition; the reverse may well be the rule.
There is good evidence that in food-producing groups
which relied too heavily on cereal and root crops,
dietary deficiencies developed, particularly those
related to vitamin deficiencies (Brothwell, 1969).
Vitamin D deficiency, resulting from excessive reliance on high carbohydrate diets, might produce
rickets in children and osteomalacia in adults, particularly in regions of low sunlight. Other vitamin
deficiencies could result in night blindness and
pellagra. Polishing rice leads to beriberi through
loss of thiamine. Iodine insufficiency in more
sedentary communities might cause thyroid malfunction.
The dependence on cultivated plants often also
bears a higher risk of famine, with its related high
mortality rates among infants and the aged; included
in this category, among groups unaccustomed to gathering wild foods or unfamiliar with a new territory, is
a greater risk of food poisoning (see Scudder, 1971,
for a recent African illustration). The use of domesticated plant foods also seems to have brought about

increase in the prevalence of dental caries, produced by diets high in carbohydrates, though this process was gradual and became important only long after food production was first adopted (Brothwell, 1969). Finally, increased tooth wear, particularly on the molars, is often correlated with greater consumption of silica-bearing grains and of the stone debris incorporated when grinding or pounding the grains in querns or mortars.

At times, food production caused more basic biological changes involving the genetic structure of the population. Such changes may have resulted in part from new conditions of gene exchange as extreme exogamy became less necessary with higher population density. If the rate of gene flow was decreased with food production as greater local endogamy prevailed, there might be less genetic variability or plasticity; this stabilization due to inbreeding could be a factor in the creation of some of the existing racial groups (Owen, 1965). However, this might be only the speeding up of a process that was already under way in the late Pleistocene; and in any case it might be argued that the inbreeding would tend to be offset by the increasing network of cultural (and, presumably, genetic) exchanges resulting from increasing intergroup contacts following the adoption of food production (Shatin, 1967). Given the ecological and cultural diversity, the real situation was probably too complicated to be subsumed under a single rule.

Use of animal milk products in some regions of the Old World probably created selective pressures that favored the genotype for adult lactase production in some groups, especially Caucasians and some Africans. Populations in overcrowded regions subject to periodic crop failure might become "famine adapted" for smaller body size and smaller calorie needs (Brothwell, 1969, p. 542). Some agricultural populations in tropical zones, with reduced animal protein intake and consequent shortage of some essential amino acids, seem also to have become miniaturized as large body size became maladaptive—

probably through man's inherent growth plasticity rather than through true genetic adaptation, however (Stini, 1971). Certainly after Pleistocene times, the weakening of some hitherto strong selective pressure—perhaps hunting?—permitted the existing wide range in human body stature, from pygmy size to over six feet, to come about. In contrast, the Paleolithic size range, as indicated by skeletons, was usually between five and six feet in height (Washburn and Lancaster, 1968, p. 295). The increase in food production may also have led to an increase in the distribution of the male sex-linked red-green color blindness, perhaps again as selective pressures related to hunting relaxed (Post, 1962). There seems to have been a reduction in the size of the incisors with the coming of food production. The smallest teeth today are found among those groups whose ancestors have had food production the longest. With this reduction apparently goes a disappearance of shovel-shaped incisors, which were common in Paleolithic times (Brace and Montagu, 1965, pp. 301-302). The reduction seems to be related to changes in food preparation techniques and to the decreased need to use the teeth for purposes other than eating. Perhaps the dental overbite so frequent in modern man is also related in some way to the new diets and new eating habits (Brace and Mahler, 1971). Whether the phenomenon of increasing roundheadedness since Pleistocene times is related, directly or indirectly, to food production is still unknown. However, with the development and spread of intensive agriculture, thin skulls became common in both hemispheres (Hulse, 1971, p. 429).

A final point on the effects of the new food-producing way of life on man's biology concerns the way in which the new social and cultural forms may have repressed some basic psychological and biological processes that had developed in the early stages of the human career, during the several million years of partial or extensive dependence on hunting as a way of life. The argument, based on physiological and psychological research in recent years, is that under the earlier conditions man had developed biological responses to situations of emergency or stress that are malfunctional today.   The human adrenal glands were adapted to mobilizing the bodies of hunters to immediate activity in times of crisis, or to spurts of energy during fatigue; extra quantities of hormones, injected into the bloodstream, released fatty products to produce energy for the muscles.   Under sedentary, food-producing conditions—and particularly for modern man, who often finds a social premium attached to the control of impulses and emotions—the fat in human tissues is not used up.   Instead, it circulates in the bloodstream with cholesterol to clog the arteries and often produce coronary heart disease (Howell, 1967, pp. 172-173).   The hypothesis is attractive and may very well be a valid interpretation of one more consequence of the shift from foraging conditions since the end of the Pleistocene.

Chapter 10
The Redistribution of Races
and Languages

Whether or not the majority of the existing biological groups that we sometimes categorize as "races" developed in the late Pleistocene or with the advent of food production, it seems true that food production drastically altered their original geographical distributions and relative demographic importance (see Brothwell, 1969; Brace and Montagu, 1965). As food producing was adopted by peoples in the areas where it first developed, the resulting pressures on resources caused not only local expansion into little-used habitats, but also diffusion into more distant and less populated regions. As we have already mentioned, agriculturalists typically have more highly organized societies, with the capacity to develop considerable military power; this would aid in the penetration of new regions.

The result in many instances was an important shift in genetic distributions throughout the world. Groups that had presumably been long dominant in certain regions during Pleistocene and preagricultural times were now swamped by newcomers, and they were generally exterminated, absorbed genetically and culturally, or pushed into regions where they did not compete with the food producers. The Bushmen and related Khoisan groups, who during the late Pleistocene in southern Africa may have been as numerous as or more numerous than the presumably "white" populations

of contemporary Upper Paleolithic Europe, North
Africa, and the Near East, were reduced to an insignificant minority status with the spread of food producers. Undoubtedly the Caucasoids increased greatly
in numbers following their head start in food producing, just as they did again between 1800 and 1930
following the Industrial Revolution in Europe (see
Cipolla, 1964, p. 102). In Asia, the Mongoloids may
originally have been restricted to northern China,
Mongolia, and adjacent regions; with the adoption of
cultivated plants, and especially of rice, they seem
to have spread into Southeast Asia and the East
Indies. The various sea migrations into Oceania,
including Polynesia, probably represent extensions of
this movement. The Ainu of Japan, who may represent
the remnants of an earlier stock that inhabited much
of eastern Asia, seem to have been restricted to
northern Japan, beyond the limits of cultivation of
premodern varieties of rice, by the arrival of the
ancestors of the Japanese. With food production, the
populations of Mesoamerica and Peru increased to numbers that may have exceeded those of the rest of the
New World. African black populations, which are
thought to have developed in the savanna area between
the Sahara and the rain forests, were able with the
adoption of domesticated plants and animals and the
use of iron tools to expand throughout sub-Saharan
Africa. The inevitable gene exchanges that occurred
during these racial expansions resulted in the many
mixed groups known today. We cannot say that in preagricultural times the world was everywhere marked by
neat, well-defined boundaries of physical types and
traits, but it is probably true that food production
accelerated the process of worldwide genetic recombi-
nation that has become even more intensive in the
past few centuries. Although many small and perhaps
unique isolates may have disappeared without trace,
there is perhaps more overall genetic diversity in
the world today than ever before in human history.
     Food production must have had similar repercus-
sions on the distribution of linguistic groups. Many

of the late preagricultural languages must have vanished or been severely reduced in relative importance. Among those that seem to have lost ground are
the click languages of Africa spoken by Bushmen and
Hottentots, the Ainu language of Japan, many languages of Australia and New Guinea, and perhaps some
of the residual languages of the New World. In contrast, the enormous expansion (geographical as well
as numerical) of such language groups as Uto-Aztecan,
Indo-European, Malayo-Polynesian, Sino-Tibetan, and
Bantu, which originally were probably no more significant than many that have vanished or been reduced,
reflects one further consequence of the differential
adaptation to food production of the early populations.

Today, as a result of the events deriving from
the expansion of food production, only a tiny scat-
tering of hunters and gatherers remains in the world—
about twenty-seven main groups altogether, repre-
senting an unknown number of individuals whose fu-
tures are bleak. The most important groups are the
Bushmen and Pygmies of Africa, the negritos of southeastern Asia, the hunters of Siberia and India, the
aboriginal Australians, the Eskimos, the Athapaskans,
and various bands of tropical South America (see
Murdock, 1968, for a useful catalogue of recent
hunters and gatherers). They have survived so far
because they live in isolated areas of low agricultural potential. They are witnesses to the fact that
food production ultimately created a world in which
hunting and gathering no longer provide a viable or
tolerable means of livelihood. In evolutionary perspective, there has been a long-range process of
selection against those who managed for so long to
hold out against the mixed blessings of the new life
and to avoid what one writer calls "those first fatal
steps toward the primrose-lined, ambition-greased,
chute of civilization" (Bates, 1952, p. 53). Food-
producers, because of their larger numbers, their
more complex and tighter social and political forms,
their ability to be more sedentary than most hunter-

gatherers, their more advanced technology, and their control of greater sources of energy, have been able to take over most of the earth in the relatively short period of ten thousand years.

Nonetheless, although nothing has yet replaced food production based on agriculture as a worldwide basis of subsistence, the Industrial Revolution has cut deeply into the proportion of the world's population engaged in agriculture—from more than 80 percent in 1750 to about 60 percent in 1950, according to one authority, and falling rapidly. Indeed, this economist has predicted that "the day may not be too distant when the proportion of farmers in the world will be no larger than the proportion of hunters in the late eighteenth century" (Cipolla, 1964, p. 25). Human cultures, like biological organisms, are so constructed that they tend to develop selective advantages which enable those with more advanced organization to submerge or eliminate their predecessors. It is thus conceivable that the forms of food production we have known since the Neolithic will be replaced in turn, at some time in the future, by forms based on very different principles, such as direct synthesis by chemical or other means that bypass the normal plant and animal converters of solar energy. It is hard for us today to envision the social and political changes this might bring about, although in the Western world in the last century we have had a glimpse of the disruptive effects of a fairly gradual reduction in numbers of the rural farming population.

Chapter 11
An Evaluation

It is difficult to evaluate a transformation which is so recent and so profound that we are still reacting to its effects. This is all the more true when we reflect that, in the anthropological perspective of man's total prehistory, a commitment to dependence on food production and to life organized according to its exigencies appears as a deviation, almost an aberration, in human behavior. Perhaps only the Paleolithic archaeologist accustomed to studying the very slowly changing, highly stable cultures of the Pleistocene is fully adapted to appreciate this fact, and even he may sometimes lose sight of the magnitude and significance of the events that occurred in early Holocene times.

In most of the world since then, mankind has been propelled in a path determined by the accelerative innovations resulting from food production. During prehistoric times the movements and shifts were slow and often difficult to recognize. In the historic period, particularly in the past few centuries, the effects have become telescoped and all too obvious. The population growth, resource depletion, and planetary pollution that worry us today have their roots in the change that occurred in prehistoric times. So do the institutions of organized conflict and warfare, and the systematic exploitation of one human group by another. Probably, many of the

prevalent and conflicting world views and deep philosophical and moral convictions that exist today go
back to the processes that shaped the peoples and
their habitats during those times. Certainly the
remarkable degree of biological and cultural conti-
nuity from prehistoric to recent times in some parts
of the world—China, the Near East, Africa, and much
of Latin America—supports the notion that the basic
ground rules for many thriving modern agriculture-
based societies were established during their earlier
food-producing periods.

If, for the sake of convenience, human culture
is regarded as a single system, a functioning entity
whose parts are all interrelated, then clearly its
different components are affected in dissimilar ways
by new forms of adaptation. This is an obvious
correlate of a holistic view of cultures and societies, but defining specific interrelationships and
changes is always much more easily discussed in theory
than demonstrated in practice. Some effects are direct and immediate, but subtle side effects may in the
long run be even more significant. I think this has
often been the case in the development of food production. This is one reason it is so difficult to
produce a tidy, consistent evaluation of the processes and events involved. The aim of this book has
been to suggest, in a necessarily abbreviated way,
how the various components of cultures in general—
technological, economic, social and political, religious and aesthetic, linguistic, and biological—were
enlarged and in many cases altered. I am not certain
of the extent to which we can generalize about the
rate and importance of the changes in each category,
and I have tried to avoid such facile generalizations.
We know, of course, that settlement patterns and subsistence activities underwent considerable changes;
that technology was variable in its degree of change,
but tended toward greater complexity and more control
of nonhuman energy; and that social organization was
probably flexible but showed trends toward certain
definable forms, depending on group size and

permanence and on productivity. Beyond these simple generalizations we have not yet carefully explored the consequences of food production on the various components of society, particularly in the cognitive and ideological domains. This remains a worthwhile field of research, to the evolutionary aspects of which archaeologists can presumably make some contributions.

The term "revolution" to describe what happened in many parts of the world when food production was established has fallen out of fashion somewhat in recent years. For some, the word is too dramatic or flamboyant; for others, it seems too explosive to describe what they see as a gradual process which may go back in some forms well into the Pleistocene. If one accepts the viewpoint, increasingly promulgated these days by some prehistorians, that the origins of domestication and cultivation are to be found in the Paleolithic, then one is justified in saying (as the historian de Tocqueville remarked about political revolutions) that the Neolithic revolution only validated what had already occurred. Nevertheless, when we look at the sudden changes against the background of the relatively stable Pleistocene sequence, particularly in the Old World, the term "revolution" does seem more appropriate than "evolution." In the technical sense of a bursting out of forces previously held in restraint by other forces, food production does entail a cultural explosion. A great deal changed in a very short time. The Near East, for instance, leaped from band society to bureaucracy in a few thousand years. In the sense that it was a relatively rapid set of innovative changes producing a state of affairs from which a return to the previous state was virtually impossible, it was a revolution. We do not yet understand very well the course of this revolution, but it is obvious that food production, whatever its tempo of development, marks the great dividing line in human affairs up to now—in my opinion, an even more significant event than the appearance of hominids of *sapiens* type in the latter

half of the Pleistocene. Morgan was right when,
nearly a century ago, he contended that man's achievements as a food-producing barbarian "should be considered in their relation to the sum of human progress; and we may be forced to admit that they tran-
scend, in relative importance, all his subsequent
works" (Morgan, 1877, p. 31).

To the archaeologist as an anthropologist, the
search for cause-and-effect relationships, for associations and correlations, for generalizations and
regularities constitutes a major part of his objec-
tives. But for other scholars—those on the receiving
end of archaeological investigations—it is the results and attainment of the research, especially per-
taining to their own fields, that represent the contributions of archaeology and the opportunity to
extract meaning, if such is possible, from the rec-
ords of the past. This is particularly true for those
disciplines which study man, for as the British social
anthropologist Needham recently put it (1973), the
supreme question which lies behind every humane disci-
pline is: What is the nature of human existence?
This is not merely a metaphysical question, and it
may not be pretentious to think that even a study of
the circumstances of early food production may help
us along the path to understanding the human situation.

In the first place, it is increasingly difficult
to fit the archaeological and other data into a tele-
ological framework and to see in the beginnings of
food production and the resulting changes any long-
term intent or purposeful behavior on the part of man
in general or specific human groups in particular.
Much of what might seem, with the benefit of hindsight, to be purposeful behavior impelled by some
inherent tendency toward complexity and progress, was
more likely the side effects of short-run adaptations
that in the long run proved selectively advantageous
for the innovating groups. As already suggested, food
production in its initial stage probably represented
merely a series of technical innovations adopted or
developed to maintain the status quo rather than to
abolish it. After a fairly successful muddle through

the Pleistocene by other short-run adaptations, it
was neither human intent nor external interference
that induced a series of small changes which, almost
without warning, changed the rules of the game. In
this respect, early food production can be seen as
an illustration of what is sometimes called Romer's
Rule in paleontology: the initial survival value of
a favorable innovation lies in the fact that it
renders possible the maintenance of a traditional
pattern of life in changed circumstances. The original Neolithic revolutionists were conservative oppor-
tunists, like many political revolutionaries and like
natural selection itself.

A second line of thinking concerns the survival
value of the new adaptation—whether it has been more
successful, in terms of stress, welfare, and dura-
tion, than the one based on hunting and collecting
that it supplanted. We touch here on a question about
which many philosophers, reformers, and even anthropologists have speculated: what is the real nature
of man's Age of Gold, the time in his career when he
was, if not innocent, at least at one with nature?
Speculators have disagreed on just when this happy
age occurred, however. Some have seen it in the time
when man lived as a hunter and gatherer, when his
social systems "based upon kinship and characterized
by liberty, equality, and fraternity were unquestionably more congenial to the human primate's
nature, and more compatible with his psychic needs
and aspirations, than any other that has ever been
realized in any of the cultures subsequent to the
Agricultural Revolution, including our own society
today" (White, 1959, p. 278). Much earlier, in 1755,
Rousseau had argued the same case, that wheat cultivation and iron metallurgy produced the "great revolution" that ruined humanity: equality disappeared,
slavery and misery grew, property was introduced, and
work became indispensable. Recently two anthropologists have argued that the agricultural revolution was
"the great leap backward," returning man to the re-
strictive drudgery of our primate past before hunting
developed as a way of life (Tiger and Fox, 1971, p. 126).
But other scholars have preferred a later chronology.

Lévi-Strauss, although in many ways a neo-Rousseauian, thinks that the Neolithic way of life offers the closest resemblance to mankind in a state of nature, and that perhaps man would have been happier if he had maintained this state (Lévi-Strauss, 1955, p. 452). Arnold Toynbee (1973) seems to have a similar view.

Unquestionably, without the development of societies fully committed to agriculture within the past ten thousand years, our world would be very different. It would be inhabited by hunters, gatherers, and fishermen, for the most part nomadic and thinly spread on the landscape, with small concentrations of more sedentary tribal groups in some of the favored corners. Many islands would probably still be unoccupied. The racial distributions of man would differ greatly from those of today. Forms of art and religion we can hardly imagine might be prevalent. Many aspects of the physical environment would undoubtedly be better. Perhaps, as some believe, life would be more satisfying for the individual in spite of its precariousness and hardships. On this point each person must make his own decision—a decision usually determined, I suspect, by his own temperament.

In defense of the view that would locate the idyllic past among the early village farmers rather than among the hunters and gatherers, it has been argued that food production, despite all its drawbacks, has permitted the growth of societies that have enlarged man's capacity to be human. Certainly the events of the past ten millennia have revealed facets of man's cultural potentiality, favorable and otherwise, that a Pleistocene observer would have found inconceivable. The idea of cultural progress has fallen into disrepute since the optimistic days of the nineteenth century; we are no longer sure how to define it, or whether it really exists. However, if we choose as one criterion of progress in human history the classic liberal concept of the degree to which individuals have been freed from the constraints imposed by environment and technology and enabled to develop more of their own capacities, then,

perhaps, we must agree with such writers as the prehistorian Childe (1944) that food production marks a
progressive event in human cultural evolution. For
better or for worse, food production has created patterns of culture that have, to borrow Geertz's words
(1964), "actualized" and not merely "constrained"
human nature.

The other side of this coin is less cheering,
however; it involves the capacity of man to continue
living in what is sometimes called the "human niche."
There is no shortage these days of either Cassandras
prophesying universal doom or optimists hawking
technological fixes for each crisis. For most of us,
it is difficult to locate ourselves on the continuum
between apocalyptic doom-saying on the one extreme
and senseless euphoria on the other. But one fact is
self-evident. Whatever catastrophes the pre-food-
producing populations of the world were exposed to,
it is highly unlikely that once *Homo sapiens sapiens*
had dispersed throughout the earth as an accomplished
hunter-gatherer, he was ever in any real danger of
extinguishing himself or destroying his milieu. In
the twentieth century man has achieved that capacity,
and the shadow of this threat may never be lifted.
Today we can seriously ask whether man and the global
environment are any longer compatible. This is
surely the most paradoxical and ironic of all the
consequences that have flowed from the development of
food production—which, it has been argued here, was
initially an adaptation for maintaining as much as
possible of the old order of things.

For some years now I have been excavating a site
in the Zagros mountains of Iran, in the heart of the
region where Near Eastern food-producing societies
emerged. The mound dates to nearly ten thousand
years ago; it represents a sequence of hamlets, each
probably containing a few dozen people who were just
developing the techniques of agriculture and more or
less sedentary life: domesticated goats, cereals,
houses of sun-dried brick, simple pottery. In these
communities and in a few others like them now being

excavated, we can truly say: This is where and how
it all began; this is the embryo of our own world.
It is irrestibly tempting to archaeologists, as they
study these humble remains with the privilege of
hindsight and with an awareness of subsequent culture
history, to wonder whether these people of the early
Holocene were taking the "right" turning after all.
I still do not know the answer to this question, but,
even at the risk of committing the *post hoc* fallacy,
it is increasingly hard to avoid the feeling that,
given man's reproductive capacities and the nature of
food production itself, the major consequences were
inescapable.

Notes

1. Triticale, the first viable new species of cereal produced since the Neolithic, was developed only in the past century by plant geneticists as a cross between wheat and rye. Other synthetic species are now being attempted, such as crosses between wheat and barley, and between barley and rye.

2. Readers interested in more detailed discussions of the origins of food production and of the various domesticates and cultigens should consult Harris (1967; 1972), Harlan (1971), Zeuner (1963), and especially the articles in Ucko and Dimbleby (1969) and Braidwood and Willey (1962). The ecology of food production is discussed by Flannery (1973), Higgs (1972), Netting (1974), and Sauer (1969). For interesting examples of ecology-oriented approaches to the problems of initial food production in Mesoamerica and Mesopotamia, respectively, see Byers (1967) and Hole, Flannery, and Neeley (1969). Other useful treatments occur in Struever (1971) and Butzer (1971). Regional syntheses of the early stages of agriculture are given in the following: for the Near East, Braidwood (1975), Mellaart (1965), and Singh (1974); for Africa, Clark (1970) and Shaw (1972); for Egypt, Clark (1971); for Europe, Piggott (1965); for the Indian subcontinent, Allchin and Allchin (1968); for China, Chang (1968); for east Asia in general, Chang (1970); for North and Central America, Willey (1966) and

Sanders and Price (1968); for South America, especially Peru, Willey (1971), Lanning (1967), and
Patterson (1973).

3. This is by no means a novel idea. It has been
suggested by many writers in the past, such as the
Scottish philosopher Lord Kames in the late eighteenth
century (Slotkin, 1965, p. 424) and by some of his
contemporaries.

4. One issue I shall not pursue further is why animals and plants were domesticated in the first place.
Although a basically economic explanation (or preju-
dice) is favored here, it is only fair to mention
that some serious writers, such as Isaac (1970), re-
ject this approach and prefer a currently unfashion-
able one based on religious motivations (see also
Sauer, 1969). Some of the arguments for that view
are by no means unattractive.

5. It is not likely that all the claimed hunter-
gatherer villages in the early Holocene in southwest
Asia were in fact without food production. Often
these claims are based on negative evidence or on
ambiguous faunal or floral materials. Already several such villages have been shown to have possessed
cultivated or domesticated foods.

6. This situation is not entirely clear at present,
however. Very simple, soft pottery was undoubtedly
present in many sites lacking the proper physical
conditions for its survival and archaeological discovery. In southwest Asia, pottery may go back some way
beyond the ca. 7000 B.C. date recently established at
a site in Iran (Smith, 1971). In Japan it is now
known, apparently in a nonagricultural context, about
11,000 B.C. In any case, much depends on the definition one selects for food production, and where
one places its beginnings.

7. This was not universally true, however. In some
cases, as in New Guinea, the change from hunting-

gathering to food production in prehistoric times seems to have involved few or no changes in the stone tool-kits.

8.   But the "Big-Man" system of Melanesia shows that leaders may expend their wealth for prestige rather than passing it on to their descendants.

9.   It is not unlikely that some advance Palaeolithic hunting-gathering groups of the late Pleistocene also utilized some astronomical devices for determining seasonal changes and predicting animal and plant availability, although such devices may have involved small portable "calculators" in bone or stone rather than large fixed stations.

References

Aberle, David F. (1961). "Matrilineal descent in cross-cultural perspective." In David M. Schneider and Kathleen Gough, eds., *Matrilineal Kinship*, pp. 655-727. Berkeley and Los Angeles: University of California Press.

Adams, Robert McC. (1966). *The Evolution of Urban Society: Early Mesopotamia and Prehispanic Mexico*. Chicago: Aldine.

Albers, Patricia, and Seymour Parker (1971). "The Plains vision experience: a study of power and privilege." *Southwestern Journal of Anthropology*, 27(3):203-233.

Allchin, Bridget, and Raymond Allchin (1968). *The Birth of Indian Civilization*. Harmondsworth, England: Penguin.

Anderson, Robert T. (1971). "Voluntary associations in history." *American Anthropologist*, 73: 209-222.

Angel, J. Lawrence (1966). "Porotic hyperostosis, anemias, malarias, and marshes in the prehistoric eastern Mediterranean." *Science*, 153:760-763.

Barrau, Jacques (1958). *Subsistence Agriculture in Melanesia*. Honolulu: B. P. Bishop Museum Bulletin, 219.

Barry, Herbert, Irving Child, and Margaret K. Bacon (1959). "Relation of child training to subsistence economy." *American Anthropologist*, 61:51-63.

Bartholomew, George A., Jr., and Joseph B. Birdsell
(1953). "Ecology and the protohominids." *American Anthropologist*, 55:481-498.

Bates, Marston (1952). *Where Winter Never Comes*.
New York: Scribner's.

Binford, Lewis R. (1968a). "Post-Pleistocene
adaptations." In S. R. Binford and L. R. Binford,
eds., *New Perspectives in Archaeology*, pp. 313-341. Chicago: Aldine.

Binford, Lewis R. (1968b). "Methodological considerations of the archaeological use of ethnographic data." In Richard B. Lee and Irven DeVore,
eds., *Man the Hunter*, pp. 268-273. Chicago:
Aldine.

Birdsell, Joseph B. (1968). "Some predictions for
the Pleistocene based on equilibrium systems among
recent hunter-gatherers." In Richard B. Lee and
Irven DeVore, eds., *Man the Hunter*, pp. 229-240.
Chicago: Aldine.

Black, Francis L. (1975). "Infectious diseases in
primitive societies." *Science*, 187:515-518.

Boserup, Ester (1965). *The Conditions of Agricultural Growth. The Economics of Agrarian Change
under Population Pressure*. London: George Allen
and Unwin.

Boserup, Ester (1970). *Woman's Role in Economic
Development*. New York: St. Martin's Press.

Brace, C. L., and Mahler, P. E. (1971). "Post-
Pleistocene changes in the human dentition.
American Journal of Physical Anthropology, 34(2):
191-204.

Brace, C. Loring, and M. F. Ashley Montagu (1965).
*Man's Evolution: An Introduction to Physical
Anthropology*. New York: Macmillan.

Braidwood, Robert J. (1975). *Prehistoric Men*. 8th
ed. Glenview, Ill.: Scott, Foresman.

Braidwood, Robert J., et al. (1953). "Did man once
live by beer alone?" *American Anthropologist*,
55:515-526.

Braidwood, Robert J., and Bruce Howe (1960). *Prehistoric Investigations in Iraqi Kurdistan.* Chicago: Oriental Institute Studies in Ancient Oriental Civilization, 31.

Braidwood, Robert J., and Charles A. Reed (1957). "The achievement and early consequences of food-production: a consideration of the archaeological and natural-historical evidence." *Cold Spring Harbor Symposia on Quantitative Biology,* 22:19-31.

Braidwood, Robert J., and Gordon R. Willey, eds. (1962). *Courses Toward Urban Life.* New York: Viking Fund Publications in Anthropology, 32.

Brothwell, Don R. (1969). "Dietary variations and the biology of earlier human populations." In Peter J. Ucko and G. W. Dimbleby, eds., *The Domestication and Exploitation of Plants and Animals,* pp. 531-545. London: Duckworth.

Brown, Judith K. (1970). "A note on the division of labor by sex." *American Anthropologist,* 72:1073-1078.

Butzer, Karl W. (1971). *Environment and Archaeology.* 2nd ed. Chicago: Aldine.

Byers, Douglas S., ed. (1967). *The Prehistory of the Tehuacan Valley, Vol. I: Environment and Subsistence.* Austin: University of Texas Press.

Campbell, Joseph (1959). *The Masks of God. Primitive Mythology.* New York: Viking.

Carneiro, Robert L. (1967). "On the relationship between size of population and complexity of social organization." *Southwestern Journal of Anthropology,* 23:234-243.

Carneiro, Robert L. (1970). "A theory of the origin of the state." *Science,* 169:733-738.

Carneiro, Robert L., and Daisy F. Hilse (1966). "On determining the probable rate of population growth during the Neolithic." *American Anthropologist,* 68:177-180.

Chang, Kwang-chih (1968). *The Archaeology of Ancient China.* Rev. ed. New Haven: Yale University Press.

Chang, Kwang-chih (1970). "The beginnings of agri-
culture in the Far East." *Antiquity*, 44:175-185.
Charney, Jules, Peter M. Stone, and William J. Quirk
(1975). "Drought in the Sahara: a biogeophysical
feedback mechanism." *Science*, 187:434-435.
Childe, V. Gordon (1936). *Man Makes Himself*.
London: Watts.
Childe, V. Gordon (1941). "War in prehistoric
societies." *The Sociological Review*, 33:126-138.
Childe, V. Gordon (1942). *What Happened in History*.
Harmondsworth, England: Penguin.
Childe, V. Gordon (1944). *Progress and Archaeology*.
London: Thinker's Library.
Childe, V. Gordon (1950). "The urban revolution."
Town Planning Review, 21:3-17.
Childe, V. Gordon (1953). "Old World prehistory:
Neolithic." In Alfred L. Kroeber, ed., *Anthro-
pology Today*, pp. 193-210. Chicago: University of
Chicago Press.
Childe, V. Gordon (1954). "Early forms of society."
In C. S. Singer, E. J. Holmyard, and A. R. Hall,
eds., *A History of Technology*, I, pp. 38-57.
Oxford: Clarendon Press.
Cipolla, Carlo M. (1964). *The Economic History of
World Population*, Rev. ed. Harmondsworth, England:
Penguin.
Clark, Colin (1963). "Agricultural productivity in
relation to population." In G. Wolstenholme, ed.,
Man and his Future, pp. 23-25. London: Churchill.
Clark, Colin, and Margaret Haswell (1967). *The
Economics of Subsistence Agriculture*, 3rd ed. New
York: St. Martin's Press.
Clark, J. Desmond (1970). *The Prehistory of Africa*.
London: Thames and Hudson.
Clark, J. Desmond (1971). "A re-examination of the
evidence for agricultural origins in the Nile
Valley." *Proceedings of the Prehistoric Society*,
37(2):34-79.
Clark, J. G. D. (1952). *Prehistoric Europe: The
Economic Basis*. New York: Philosophical Library.

Clark, J. G. D. (1966). "Prehistory and human be-
havior." *Proceedings of the American Philosophical
Society*, 111(2):91-98.
Cockburn, T. Aidan (1971). "Infectious diseases in
ancient populations." *Current Anthropology* 12:45-
62.
Dixon, J. E., J. R. Cann, and C. Renfrew (1968).
"Obsidian and the origins of trade." *Scientific
American*, 218:38-46.
Douglas, Mary (1969). "Is matriliny doomed in
Africa?" In M. Douglas and P. M. Kaberry, eds.,
Man in Africa, pp. 121-135. London: Tavistock.
Douglas, Mary (1974). "Food as an art form." *Studio:
International Journal of Modern Art*, 188:83-88.
Drucker, Philip, and Robert F. Heizer (1967). *To
Make My Name Good*. Berkeley and Los Angeles:
University of California Press.
Dumond, Don E. (1975). "The limitation of human
population: a natural history." *Science*, 187:
713-721.
Dunn, Frederick L. (1968). "Epidemiological factors:
health and disease in hunter-gatherers." In
Richard B. Lee and Irven DeVore, eds., *Man the
Hunter*, pp. 221-228. Chicago: Aldine.
Edgerton, Robert B. (1965). "'Cultural' vs.
'ecological' factors in the expression of values,
attitudes and personality characteristics."
American Anthropologist, 67:442-447.
Eliade, Mircea (1960). "Structures and changes in the
history of religion." In C. H. Kraeling and R. M.
Adams, eds., *City Invincible*, pp. 351-366. Chicago:
University of Chicago Press.
Engels, Frederick (1884). *Origin of the Family,
Private Property, and the State*. Zurich: Hottigen
(in German).
Flannery, Kent V. (1969). "Origins and ecological
effects of early domestication in Iran and the Near
East." In P. J. Ucko and G. W. Dimbleby, eds., *The
Domestication and Exploitation of Plants and
Animals*, pp. 73-100. London: Duckworth.

Flannery, Kent V. (1972). "The origins of the village as a settlement type in Mesoamerica and the Near East: a comparative study." In P. J. Ucko, R. Tringham, and G. W. Dimbleby, eds., *Man, Settlement and Urbanism*, pp. 23-53. London: Duckworth.

Flannery, Kent V. (1973). "The origins of agriculture." In B. J. Siegel, A. R. Beals and S. A. Tyler, eds., *Annual Review of Anthropology*, 2, pp. 271-310. Palo Alto: Annual Reviews, Inc.

Fried, Morton H. (1967). *The Evolution of Political Society*. New York: Random House.

Galbraith, John Kenneth (1967). *The New Industrial State*. New York: Houghton, Mifflin.

Geertz, Clifford (1964). "The transition to humanity." In Sol Tax, ed., *Horizons of Anthropology*, pp. 37-48. Chicago: Aldine.

Goggin, John M., and William C. Sturtevant (1964). "The Calusa: a stratified, non-agricultural society" (with notes on sibling marriage). In Ward H. Goodenough, ed., *Explorations in Cultural Anthropology: Essays in Honor of George Peter Murdock*, pp. 179-219. New York: McGraw-Hill.

Goldschmidt, Walter (1959). *Man's Way*. Cleveland: World.

Goldschmidt, Walter (1965). "Theory and strategy in the study of cultural adaptability." *American Anthropologist*, 67:402-408.

Gould, Harold A. (1971). *Caste and Class: A Comparative View*. Reading, Mass.: Addison-Wesley Modular Publications, 11.

Harlan, Jack R. (1967). "A wild wheat harvest in Turkey." *Archaeology*, 20:197-201.

Harlan, Jack R. (1971). "Agricultural origins: centers and noncenters." *Science*, 174:468-474.

Harris, David R. (1967). "New light on plant domestication and the origins of agriculture: a review." *Geographical Review*, 57:90-107.

Harris, David R. (1972). "The origins of agriculture in the tropics." *American Scientist*, 60(2):180-193.

Hatch, Marion P. (1971). "An hypothesis on Olmec astronomy, with special reference to the La Venta site." *Contributions to the University of California Research Facility*, 13 (Papers on Olmec and Maya Archeology), pp. 1-63.

Haudricourt, A. (1970). "Aspects qualitatifs des civilisations agricoles de la société de communauté primitive." In *VII Congrès International des Sciences Anthropologiques et Ethnologiques*, Moscow, 1964, Vol. 5, pp. 506-507.

Hawkins, Gerald (1965). *Stonehenge Decoded*. London: Souvenir Press.

Heizer, Robert F. (1955). "Primitive man as an ecologic factor." *Kroeber Anthropological Society Papers*, 13:1-31.

Heizer, Robert F. (1958). "Prehistoric central California: a problem in historical-developmental classification." *University of California Archaeological Survey*, Report 41:19-26.

Heizer, Robert F. (1966). "Ancient heavy transport, methods and achievements." *Science*, 153:821-830.

Helbaek, Hans (1970). "The plant husbandry of Hacilar: a study of cultivation and domestication." In J. Mellaart, *Excavations at Hacilar*, Vol. 1, pp. 189-249. Edinburgh: University Press.

Higgs, Eric S., ed. (1972). *Papers in Economic Prehistory*. Cambridge: University Press.

Higgs, Eric S., and Michael R. Jarman (1969). "The origins of agriculture: a reconsideration." *Antiquity*, 43:31-41.

Hole, Frank, Kent V. Flannery, and James A. Neely (1969). *Prehistory and Human Ecology of the Deh Luran Plain*. Ann Arbor: University of Michigan Museum of Anthropology, Memoir No. 1.

Holmberg, Allan R. (1950). *Nomads of the Long Bow: The Siriono of Eastern Bolivia*. Washington: Smithsonian Institution, Institute of Social Anthropology, Publication 10.

Howell, F. Clark (1967). *Early Man,* Rev. ed. New York: Time-Life.

Hulse, Frederick S. (1971). *The Human Species: An Introduction to Physical Anthropology*, 2nd ed. New York: Random House.

Isaac, Erich (1970). *Geography of Domestication*. Englewood Cliffs: Prentice-Hall.

Jarman, Michael (1971). "Culture and economy in the North Italian Neolithic." *World Archaeology*, 2: 255-265.

Kluckhohn, Clyde (1960). "The moral order in the expanding society." In C. H. Kraeling and R. M. Adams, eds., *City Invincible*, pp. 391-404. Chicago: University of Chicago Press.

Kolata, Gina B. (1974). "!Kung hunter-gatherers: feminism, diet and birth control." *Science*, 185: 932-934.

Krantz, Grover S. (1970). "Human activities and megafaunal extinctions." *American Scientist*, 28: 164-170.

Kroeber, Alfred L. (1939). *Cultural and Natural Areas of Native North America*. University of California Publications in American Archaeology and Ethnology, 38.

Kroeber, Alfred L. (1948). *Anthropology*. New York: Harcourt, Brace.

Langer, William L. (1972). "Checks on population growth: 1750-1850." *Scientific American*, 226: 93-99.

Lanning, Edward P. (1967). *Peru Before the Incas*. Englewood Cliffs, N.J.: Prentice-Hall.

Lee, Richard B. (1968). "What hunters do for a living, or, how to make out on scarce resources." In Richard B. Lee and Irven DeVore, eds., *Man the Hunter*, pp. 30-48. Chicago: Aldine.

Lee, Richard B. (1969). "!Kung Bushman subsistence: an input-output analysis." In A. P. Vayda, ed., *Environment and Cultural Behavior: Ecological Studies in Cultural Anthropology*, pp. 47-79. New York: Natural History Press.

Lee, Richard B. (1974). "Male-female residence arrangements and political power in human hunter-gatherers." *Archives of Sexual Behavior*, 3:167-173.

Lévi-Strauss, Claude (1955). *Tristes Tropiques.*
Paris: Librairie Plon.

Lévi-Strauss, Claude (1962). *La Pensée Sauvage.*
Paris: Librairie Plon.

Lévi-Strauss, Claude (1966). "The scope of anthropology." *Current Anthropology*, 7:112-123.

Lomax, Alan, and Norman Berkowitz (1972). "The evolutionary taxonomy of culture." *Science*, 177: 228-239.

MacNeish, Richard S. (1971). "Speculations about how and why food production and village life developed in the Tehaucan Valley, Mexico." *Archaeology*, 24: 307-315.

Matson, Frederick R., ed. (1965). *Ceramics and Man.* Viking Fund Publications in Anthropology, 41. New York: Wenner-Gren Foundation.

Mellaart, James (1965). *Earliest Civilizations of the Near East.* London: Thames and Hudson.

Morgan, Lewis H. (1877). *Ancient Society.* New York: Holt.

Mumford, Lewis (1960). "Concluding address." In C. H. Kraeling and R. M. Adams, eds., *City Invincible*, pp. 224-246. Chicago: University of Chicago Press.

Murdock, George P. (1957). "World ethnographic sample." *American Anthropologist*, 59:664-687.

Murdock, George P. (1964). "Cultural correlates of the regulation of premarital sex behavior." In Robert A. Manners, ed., *Processes and Patterns in Culture: Essays in Honor of Julian H. Steward,* pp. 399-410. Chicago: Aldine.

Murdock, George P. (1968). "The current status of the world's hunting and gathering peoples." In Richard B. Lee and Irven DeVore, eds., *Man the Hunter*, pp. 13-20. Chicago: Aldine.

Naroll, Raoul (1956). "A preliminary index of social development." *American Anthropologist*, 68:687-715.

Needham, Rodney (1973). "Projects and impediments." *The Times Literary Supplement*, 6 July, pp. 785-786. London.

Netting, Robert M. (1969). "Ecosystems in process: a comparative study of change in two West African societies." In David Damas, ed., *Contributions to Anthropology: Ecological Essays*. Ottawa: National Museums of Canada, Bulletin 230, pp. 102-112.

Netting, Robert M. (1971). *The Ecological Approach in Cultural Study*. Reading, Mass.: Addison-Wesley Modular Publications, 6.

Netting, Robert M. (1974). "Agrarian ecology." In B. J. Siegel, A. R. Beals, and S. A. Tyler, eds., *Annual Review of Anthropology*, 3, pp. 21-56. Palo Alto: Annual Reviews, Inc.

Newcomb, W. W., Jr. (1960). "Towards an understanding of war." In G. E. Dole and R. L. Carneiro, eds., *Essays in the Science of Culture in Honor of Leslie A. White*, pp. 317-336. New York: Crowell.

Owen, Roger C. (1965). "The patrilocal band: a linguistically and culturally hybrid social unit." *American Anthropologist*, 67:675-690.

Patterson, Thomas C. (1973). *America's Past: a New World Archaeology*. Glenview: Scott, Foresman and Company.

Piggott, Stuart (1965). *Ancient Europe*. Chicago: Aldine.

Polgar, Steven (1964). "Evolution and the ills of mankind." In Sol Tax, ed., *Horizons of Anthropology*, pp. 200-211. Chicago: Aldine.

Post, Richard H. (1962). "Population differences in red and green color vision deficiency: a review and a query on selection relaxation." *Eugenics Quarterly*, 9:131-146.

Raven, P. H., B. Berlin, and D. E. Breedlove (1971). "The origins of taxonomy." *Science*, 174:1210-1213.

Redfield, Robert (1953). *The Primitive World and its Transformations*. Ithaca, N.Y.: Great Seal Books.

Ribeiro, Darcy (1968). *The Civilizational Process*. Washington: Smithsonian Institution Press.

Rousseau, Jean-Jacques (1755). *Discours sur l'origine et les fondements de l'inégalité parmi les hommes*. Paris.

Sahlins, Marshall D. (1968a). "Notes on the original affluent society." In Richard B. Lee and Irven DeVore, eds., *Man the Hunter*, pp. 85-89. Chicago: Aldine.

Sahlins, Marshall D. (1968b). *Tribesmen*. Englewood Cliffs, N.J.: Prentice-Hall.

Sahlins, Marshall D. (1972). *Stone Age Economics*. Chicago: Aldine.

Sanday, Peggy R. (1973). "Toward a theory of the status of women." *American Anthropologist*, 75: 1682-1700.

Sanders, William T., and Barbara J. Price (1968). *Mesoamerica: The Evolution of a Civilization*. New York: Random House Studies in Anthropology.

Sauer, Carl O. (1969). *Seeds, Spades, Hearths, and Herds. The Domestication of Animals and Foodstuffs*, 2nd ed. Cambridge: M.I.T. Press.

Scudder, Thayer (1971). *Gathering among African Woodland Savannah Cultivators. A Case Study: The Gwembe Tonga*. University of Zambia, Institute for African Studies, Zambian Papers 5.

Service, Elman R. (1971). *Primitive Social Organization: An Evolutionary Perspective*, 2nd ed. New York: Random House Studies in Anthropology.

Shatin, R. (1967). "The transition from food-gathering to food-production in evolution and disease." *Vitalstoffe Zivilisationkrankheiten*, 12: 104-107.

Shaw, Thurston (1972). "Early agriculture in Africa." *Journal of the Historical Society of Nigeria*, 6:143-191.

Singh, Purushottam (1974). *Neolithic Cultures of Western Asia*. London and New York: Seminar Press.

Slotkin, J. S. (1965). *Readings in Early Anthropology*. New York: Viking Fund Publications in Anthropology, 40.

Smith, Cyril S. (1965). "Materials and the development of civilization and science." *Science*, 148: 908-917.

Smith, Philip E. L. (1971). "Iran, 9000-4000 B.C.: the Neolithic." *Expedition*, 13(3-4):6-13.

Smith, Philip E. L. (1972a). *The Consequences of Food Production*. Reading, Mass.: Addison-Wesley Modular Publications, 31.

Smith, Philip E. L. (1972b). "Changes in population pressure in archaeological explanation." *World Archaeology*, 4(1):5-18.

Smith, Philip E. L., and T. Cuyler Young, Jr. (1972). "The evolution of early agriculture and culture in Greater Mesopotamia: a trial model." In B. J. Spooner, ed., *Population Growth: Anthropological Implications*, pp. 1-59. Cambridge, Mass.: M.I.T. Press.

Solecki, Ralph S. (1971). *Shanidar: The First Flower People*. New York: Alfred A. Knopf.

Spooner, Brian (1973). *The Cultural Ecology of Pastoral Nomads*. Reading, Mass.: Addison-Wesley Modular Publications, 45.

Steward, Julian H. (1968). "Cultural ecology." In D. L. Sills, ed., *International Encyclopaedia of the Social Sciences*, 4:337-344.

Stini, William A. (1971). "Evolutionary implications of changing nutritional patterns in human populations." *American Anthropologist*, 73:1019-1030

Struever, Stuart, ed. (1971). *Prehistoric Agriculture*. Garden City, N.Y.: American Museum Sourcebooks in Anthropology.

Textor, Robert B. (1967). *A Cross-Cultural Summary*. New Haven: HRAF Press.

Thom, Alexander (1967). *Megalithic Sites in Britain*. Oxford: Clarendon.

Thomas, William L., Jr., ed. (1956). *Man's Role in Changing the Face of the Earth*. Chicago: University of Chicago Press.

Tiger, Lionel, and Fox, Robin (1971). *The Imperial Animal*. New York: Holt, Rinehart and Winston.

Thomson, George (1960). *The Foreseeable Future*. New York: Viking.

Tofler, Alvin (1970). *Future Shock*. New York: Bantam.

Toynbee, Arnold (1973). "Civilization in retreat." The Montreal *Star*, 9 January (reprinted from The *Observer*, London).

Ucko, Peter J., and G. W. Dimbleby, eds., (1969).
*The Domestication and Exploitation of Plants and
Animals.* London: Duckworth.
Vayda, Andrew (1961). "Expansion and warfare among
swidden agriculturalists." *American Anthropolo-
gist,* 63:346-358.
Vayda, Andrew P. (1971). "Phases of the process of
war and peace among the Marings of New Guinea."
Oceania, 42:1-24.
Washburn, Sherwood L., and C. S. Lancaster (1968).
"The evolution of hunting." In Richard B. Lee and
Irving DeVore, eds., *Man the Hunter,* pp. 293-303.
Chicago: Aldine.
Watson, Richard A., and Patty Jo Watson (1969). *Man
and Nature: An Anthropological Essay in Human
Ecology.* New York: Harcourt, Brace and World.
Weinberg, Alvin M. (1972). "Social institutions and
nuclear energy." *Science,* 177:27-34.
White, J. Peter (1971). "New Guinea and Australian
prehistory: the 'Neolithic problem'." In D. J.
Mulvaney and J. Golson, eds., *Aboriginal Man and
Environment in Australia,* pp. 182-195. Canberra:
Australian National University Press.
White, Leslie A. (1959). *The Evolution of Culture:
The Development of Civilization to the Fall of Rome.*
New York: McGraw-Hill.
Wilkinson, Paul F. (1972). "Oomingmak: a model for
man-animal relationships in prehistory." *Current
Anthropology,* 13:23-44.
Willey, Gordon R. (1966). *An Introduction to
American Archaeology, Vol. I: North and Middle
America.* Englewood Cliffs, N.J.: Prentice-Hall.
Willey, Gordon R. (1971). *An Introduction to
American Archaeology, Vol. II: South America.*
Englewood Cliffs, N.J.: Prentice-Hall.
Wolf, Eric (1966). *Peasants.* Englewood Cliffs, N.J.:
Prentice-Hall.
Wright, Gary A. (1969). *Obsidian Analysis and Pre-
historic Near Eastern Trade: 7500 to 3500 B.C.*
Ann Arbor: University of Michigan Museum of Anthro-
pology, Anthropological Papers, 37.

Wright, Gary A. (1974). *Archaeology and Trade.*
Reading, Mass.: Addison-Wesley Modular Publica-
tions, 49.
Wynne-Edwards, V. C. (1962). *Animal Dispersion in
Relation to Social Behaviour.* Edinburgh: Oliver
and Boyd.
Yarwood, C. E. (1970). "Man-made plant diseases."
Science, 168:218-220.
Young, T. Cuyler, Jr. (1972). "Population densities
and early Mesopotamian urbanism." In P. J. Ucko,
R. Tringham, and G. W. Dimbleby, eds., *Man, Settle-
ment and Urbanism,* pp. 827-842. London: Duckworth.
Zeuner, F. E. (1963). *A History of Domesticated
Animals.* New York: Harper and Row.

Index